TEACHING AMIDST
THE NEON PALM TREES

By

Lee Ryan Miller

ISBN: 1-4033-3185-5 (e-book)
ISBN: 1-4033-3186-3 (Paperback)

Library of Congress Control Number: 2002095497

This book is printed on acid free paper.

Printed in the United States of America
Bloomington, IN

Cover designed by George Chun-Han Wang

1stBooks - rev. 02/27/04

To Mike, for being a true friend,
when so many false ones abandoned me.

Contents

Preface

To Bob, for giving me the time and resources to complete this book, and to Simon, for teaching me that every cloud has a silver lining.
— dedication to *Retsamdros*

Those who read my novel *Retsamdros* often ask me to explain this rather mysterious dedication. I usually smile, and tell them that it is a very good story, but one that is too long to tell right now.

Finally I am ready to tell this story. It chronicles the bizarre twists of fate that led me to write *Retsamdros*. It is a love story, or at least, a story of one teacher's love for his students. It is an espionage thriller, or at least, a story of the high-stakes intrigues and political maneuvering that built up some careers and threatened to destroy others. It is a bittersweet story of one man's seemingly futile struggle to do what he thinks is right in the face of entrenched opposition by forces he does not fully understand. It is a tale of shattered illusions, values redefined, and spiritual redemption. And it is a story of truth triumphing in the end. It is my story, and I apologize for keeping you waiting so long. But I think you will find that it was worth the wait.

This story is true. I describe real people, real places, and real events. In a small number of instances, however, I have changed the names and characteristics of certain people in order to protect their privacy. Whenever I introduce such a fictionalized character, I note in the text that I will be using a pseudonym.

One last thing before we begin. This story contains a very large cast of characters, and some readers may have difficulty keeping all of them straight. For this reason I have included a list to jog your memory, the "Cast of Characters" located near the end of the book. Feel free to refer to it whenever you get confused about the identity of the characters in the text. You also can take a peek at the Epilogue to find out what became of these people. But you'll probably enjoy the story more if you wait until the end.

Acknowledgements

Many people have helped to make this a better book. I offer them all my heartfelt thanks.

Natalie Patton of the *Las Vegas Review-Journal* and Jennifer Knight of the *Las Vegas Sun* were always ready to point me in the right direction when I reached an obstacle in my research.

My lawyers, Alexander Greenfeld and Richard Segerblom, helped me to understand the legal implications of telling my story, and helped to verify the accuracy of the information that I present. Steve Sisolak, Michael Green, Linda Foreman, Calvin Chadwick, and Mark Leichty also verified the accuracy of my account.

Anita Chun and my dear wife Beth spent countless hours editing and proofreading various drafts of this manuscript, and countless more hours poring over newspaper articles to double-check my facts.

Many additional people offered helpful suggestions on how to improve the telling of this tale, including Michael Green, Carolyn Foy-Stromberg, Cindy Hauck, Jerrold Bellenger, and my parents.

Finally, George Chun-Han Wang designed a beautiful cover.

Many thanks and much love to all of you.

Prologue

Cities, like people, often have a certain aura about them, a unique energy that permeates their very being. Las Vegas's aura is unlike that of any other place on earth.

Las Vegas is the city of illusions, a magical place in which you can visit ancient Egypt, King Arthur's court, a tropical paradise, or any number of other fantasy destinations. It is the city of dreams, a place where millions go, hoping and praying that a stroke of luck will change their lives, all of them believing that they are just a roll of the dice, a deal of the cards, or a slot machine pull away from realizing all their material dreams.

Of course, most of them fail to realize their dreams. Las Vegas also is the city of broken dreams, illusions dispelled, and too often, shattered lives. It has more than its fair share of people unable to accept the fact that their dreams will remain unrealized. Their possessions end up in pawnshops, their spirits drowned in addictions, and the shells that remain often wander the streets like ghosts among the semi-invisible legions of homeless.

A powerful mixture of great hope and great disappointment permeate the aura of Las Vegas, making it a difficult place to call home. Everyone seeks shelter, in one way or another, from the intense barrage of psychic energy that assaults them with a power surpassing even that of the desert heat. Some find solace in family life, some in drugs which deaden their ability to feel, and others in religious worship. Indeed, Las Vegas has one of the highest numbers of churches per capita of any large American city.

I sought refuge in spirituality. Long ago, I had become disillusioned with the dogmas of most organized religions. I had attended Jewish, Christian, Hindu, and Buddhist religious services, but had always felt like something was lacking, that the true spiritual path was hidden somewhere beyond the shell of prejudices and rituals. As such, I gravitated toward a more esoteric spiritual path, one which permitted me to collect pieces of what I sought from many strands of religion, one which led me constantly to question and refine my beliefs, rather than swallowing unquestioningly the doctrine that I must believe X or be damned for all eternity.

It did not take much searching for me to find a Las Vegas institution that embodied this philosophy. Simon Hunt and Patti Nicholson dedicated their lives to establishing and nurturing a place where people of all spiritual beliefs could meet, discuss, and share knowledge and love. Spiritual Endeavors' motto was "Many Paths, One Destination." Somehow Simon and Patti ran a web page design business, while simultaneously hosting in their home several times per week lectures and workshops by spiritual teachers from all over the world. This organization grew by leaps and bounds, and within a short time, *www.spiritual-endeavors.org* became the largest spiritual site on the World Wide Web.

I could not believe that these two apparently ordinary people had been able to accomplish so much in just a couple of years. But they believed with all their hearts in the philosophy that you have the power to manifest in your life whatever you choose to envision.

During my first year in Las Vegas, I became heavily involved in Spiritual Endeavors, attending lectures and workshops each week, and serving the organization in a number of volunteer capacities. Simon and Patti were always very supportive of my writing efforts, confident that I would become a successful writer when I was "ready to accept this new role."

After I was hired to teach political science full-time at the Community College of Southern Nevada (CCSN), my work schedule forced me to cut back my involvement in Spiritual Endeavors. Simon was understanding and supportive, as always.

2

"I love my job," I explained to him. "I'm able to inspire people to get more involved in making our community — and the rest of the world — a better place. I probably put in twice as many hours as I need to, but the work that I'm doing is so important." I sighed. "On the other hand, sometimes I'm frustrated that I can't seem to find the time for writing any longer."

Simon placed his hand on my shoulder in a gesture of empathy. "When you're ready to resume writing," he told me, "you'll manifest the time that you need."

I smiled politely, not quite believing him.

I

Hot Pink Edifices Amidst Neon Palm Trees

The plane circled the Las Vegas Valley, affording me a bird's-eye view of my new home. We passed over barren brown mountains, beyond which lay the blue waters of Lake Mead. It seemed a bit bizarre, that patch of blue water, surrounded by lifeless brown dirt and rock, nothing growing, no green upon its shores. A little while later, I saw plenty of green. As we circled back toward the city, I saw brightly-colored squares like a painter's palette set amidst the brown desert landscape. One square glowed bright yellow, while another was a dull brown, and a third was a sickly green. They were the ponds from the sewage treatment plant. I imagined the stench they must make in the summer heat. They lay on the shore of a sea of houses stretching dozens of miles off to the mountains enclosing the western edge of the valley. As the aircraft descended toward the runway, I caught a glimpse of an enormous black pyramid, and lots of huge hotels with brightly-lit signs.

I arrived in Las Vegas on a sweltering summer afternoon. The temperature was nearly 120 degrees, which was not all that extraordinary at that time of year. It was August 1997. I had arrived in my new home. I had no job, no place to live, and only a promise to go on.

For the past year I had lived with my girlfriend, Beth, in Tokyo, where I had been teaching political science and economics at a couple of universities. The jobs had paid well. By my final semester there, I

5

was earning the equivalent of $6,000 per month. But I knew it would not last. The economics professor in me could see the decaying foundation beneath the Asian economic miracle, and could smell a nasty recession dawning amidst the cherry blossoms of spring. It was at that time that Beth had flown to Las Vegas to interview for a job with U.S. Senator Harry Reid, to be his primary liaison with the Asian American community in Nevada. The senator's chief of staff offered her the job, and Beth was able to negotiate a promise from the senator that he would make some calls on my behalf to assist me in finding a job at a college in Las Vegas.

Actually, there were only two colleges in Las Vegas: the University of Nevada, Las Vegas (UNLV) and the Community College of Southern Nevada (CCSN). Senator Reid kept his promise. One afternoon, a few weeks after we arrived in Las Vegas, Beth called me from work. She told me that the senator had arranged for me to meet with CCSN President Richard Moore, and that I should call his secretary, Joyce Tomlinson, to confirm that I would stop by the following afternoon.

I did so, and the following afternoon, I drove to the West Charleston campus of CCSN. It was one of three campuses, this one situated on the more fashionable west side of town. Moore had only been at CCSN since 1994, and he'd had the greatest impact on this campus. When I had spoken to Joyce, she had said that I would have no trouble spotting the campus. She was right. The modern buildings were painted fluorescent purple and pink, and the palm trees were festooned with lights. Some months later, when I asked CCSN history professor Mike Green about the décor at this campus, he shrugged his shoulders and replied dryly, "Moore said he had it done this way because he wanted it to blend in with the desert colors."

The early afternoon sun glinted off the black asphalt parking lot, creating shimmering mirages as I walked toward the administration building. Sweat had soaked the shirt below my jacket and tie by the time I had completed the two-minute walk.

Joyce asked me to have a seat, explaining that Moore was in a meeting. I sat there silently in the anteroom to Moore's office as Joyce did some work on her computer. After twenty minutes, the door to the inner office abruptly burst open. I jumped. So did Joyce.

Out marched a man, at least sixty years old, with a large belly bulging from beneath his polo shirt, and wisps of white hair peeking out from below a baseball cap. He hurried past me, taking no notice.

I stood up. "Dr. M—" I began.

"Oh, yeah, follow me," he said, hardly glancing in my direction as he marched out the door.

A middle-aged Latino man hurried after Moore, and at first I was unsure whether the president's order had been to me or to the other guy. I hesitated a moment and then took off after them.

I found them outside the building talking about some sort of construction project. Moore shot me a fleeting glance and said nothing. They stood there in the heat talking for several minutes. I stood about four paces away from them, not sure what to do. I wanted to yell at the old man, "Hey, I'm right here, you rude bastard—quit ignoring me!" But I needed a job, and I kept my mouth shut. Finally, Moore pulled out his cell phone and dialed. "Is Bob there?" he growled. Moore looked annoyed at the response, and hung up. Then he picked up where he had left off in his discussion with the Latino administrator, whom he called Orlando. A couple of minutes later, Moore dialed his cell phone again, and asked if Bob was back yet. Again, he looked annoyed at the response, and hung up. He talked a bit more with Orlando, and then finally turned to me. "Let's go," he barked, and took off toward the building across from us.

Neither Moore nor Orlando said a word to me as we crossed the courtyard and entered the next building. Moore led us up some stairs and into another office. He demanded that the secretary tell him where Bob was, and when she did not produce a satisfactory answer, he spun around and faced me. "I don't know where Bob is," Moore spat. "Just wait here for him." I was dumbfounded. Moore marched out the door, with Orlando chasing after him.

I stood there for a few moments, mouth open, trying to make sense of the experience. The secretary, however, did not seem the least bit surprised. I introduced myself to her. Jo Ann Zahm, the secretary, told me that "Bob" was Dr. Robert Silverman, senior vice president of CCSN. She said that he was out somewhere, and that he would meet with me as soon as he returned.

I sat down and waited, wavering between bewilderment and utter exasperation at the way Moore had behaved. About fifteen minutes later Silverman arrived. He was an obese man in his fifties with black hair and a white beard. I stood up and offered my hand. He took it in his enormous paw and shook it.

"I'm Lee Miller," I said. "Senator Reid called yesterday and scheduled an appointment for me to meet with Dr. Moore. He, uh, left me here to meet with you."

Silverman nodded noncommittally and invited me into his office. "So, what can I do for you?" he asked.

"I'm looking for a job," I said, a bit awkwardly, unnerved as I was from the encounter with Moore.

Silverman sighed. "So, tell me about yourself," he said, leaning back in his big chair.

I took a deep breath, and told him about my Ph.D. from UCLA and my experience teaching political science and economics in Tokyo. Silverman listened patiently.

"I got my Ph.D. at UCLA too," he said, grinning. My spirits rose and I smiled. Silverman's grin faded. "Unfortunately," he said, "we don't have any openings right now. But we'll keep you in mind if anything becomes available."

I thanked him, shook his hand, and left. "They just blew me off!" I grumbled to myself as I turned on the air conditioning in my car and ripped off my jacket and tie. "What a fucking waste of time!"

I was annoyed. Everyone had gone through the motions, but no one had taken me seriously. This was my career—my life—that they were treating so cavalierly.

Anger spurred me to take matters into my own hands. When I got home, I looked up the telephone numbers of the political science and economics departments at CCSN and UNLV. I called each number and asked to speak to the chair. At CCSN, both political science and economics were situated in the Department of Philosophical and Regional Studies (PRS), a bizarre agglomeration of disciplines that included history and philosophy, but neither psychology nor sociology. The department chair was named Charles Okeke. He spoke with a heavy accent, and I could only understand about half of what he said. But the part I did understand included the fact that he had no positions available, even on a part-time basis. I received the same response from the political science department chair at UNLV.

My anger by now had subsided, and quickly was morphing into despair. I had quit my job and come to Las Vegas on a hope and a promise. I had gambled, and it looked like I had lost. "Okay, this is my last shot, my one last throw of the dice," I mumbled sourly. I picked up the phone a third time and called the economics department at UNLV.

"How soon can you meet with me?" asked Dr. Bernard Malamud, the Economics Department chair.

My spirits rose. I covered the mouthpiece of the phone. "Thank God," I gasped.

It turned out that they were in great need of someone to teach introduction to macroeconomics, and the semester was set to start in one week. I met with Dr. Malamud, who told me to call him Bernie, and he was very enthusiastic about me coming to work for him. It seems that it was extremely difficult for him to find adjunct faculty, which Bernie blamed on the "ridiculously low" wages the university paid — just $3,900 for teaching two courses in one semester, or about $975 per month. I had earned nearly twice that for half as many hours as a graduate student teaching assistant at UCLA. My wages in Tokyo were, of course, many times more generous. But I needed a job, so I accepted his offer. Unfortunately for me, when Bernie contacted the dean for final approval, the dean told him that he had already finalized the budget, and that there was no funding available for my position. Bernie apologized to me over and over again. He seemed to be genuinely disappointed, and he offered me the same job for the following semester, starting in January.

However disappointed Bernie might have been, I was a hundred times more so. But what was I to do? I did not shout or curse or do anything beyond politely accepting Bernie's offer. He seemed like a decent guy, and it was not his fault that his plan had fallen through.

Now, the problem I faced was that I had no expectation of income for the next five months. I shuddered at the thought of having given up my academic career so that I could wait tables or valet cars in Las Vegas. I began to descend into a deep depression when, a few days later — less than a week before the semester was scheduled to begin — I received a call from Rita Roberts. Rita was one of the secretaries in the Philosophical and Regional Studies (PRS) department at CCSN. She said that they had an opening to teach Economics 101 at the

9

Henderson campus four times per week. She asked me to come in later that day to meet with Dr. Okeke, the department chair.

The pay at CCSN was even lower than what I had been offered at UNLV — just $3,300 spread over four months. I would have done much better waiting tables, and I considered turning down the job. But I figured that it wouldn't hurt to meet with Okeke.

I drove to the Cheyenne campus of CCSN, located the PRS office, and opened the door. The room was large, with two desks in the center, each of which contained a computer. On either side of the room was a row of doors leading to small inner offices. Rita and the other secretary had already gone home for the day.

Dr. Okeke was a black man in his forties sporting a goatee and large wire-rimmed glasses. The summer heat had reduced most professors to their shirtsleeves, but Dr. Okeke, an economist, was smartly dressed in a jacket and tie. His office was tiny, no larger than the other faculty offices in the PRS suite. He was seated before a desk overflowing with piles of paper.

"Dr. Okeke, my name is Lee Miller," I said, extending my hand.

"Oh, doctamilla," he said in a heavy Nigerian accent. He grabbed hold of my hand, and shook it. "Plehzyuhtuhmeetyu."

I had no idea what he had said to me, but assumed it to be some sort of greeting. "Pleased to meet you," I replied.

Okeke continued holding onto my hand, no longer shaking it. At a later date I found out that it is common for Nigerian men to hold hands while they speak. "Cuminsidownwidmi," he said, gesturing toward a chair next to his desk. It was covered with papers. "Oh, letmeemeksumspes!" He finally let go of my hand, and carefully moved onto his desk the pile of papers covering the chair. I sat down and put my briefcase on my lap, holding it tightly, lest Okeke try to grab my hand again.

"Noormuhli, yuhmustav a minimum fifteen graaduit credits in the subject to teach heeyuh. Yonli haf twelf, but I think we can getit OK'd, givendasitueshin."

I nodded, not quite sure exactly what he had said, but getting the impression that they were so desperate for someone to teach these classes that they were willing to bend a few rules.

"The salary is awfully low," I said. "What's the likelihood that you'll have a full-time opening sometime soon?"

Okeke sighed, and leaned toward me. "We donaveni full-time openin's right now, *but*," he said, holding up a finger, "takindisjob will reflect well onyu, if yuhwerto apply fora full-time position inda fewcha."

So, that's the way it works, I thought. I have to pay my dues working for peanuts in order to get a full-time job. I sighed. "Okay, I'll take the job."

"Vehry happy tuheerdat, doctamilla," he said, grabbing hold of my hand again. "Rita will tekeruvahl duh details. She's gone home fuhduday. You can meetwidder tomorrow."

"Thanks," I said, standing. "I appreciate the opportunity." I pulled my hand from his grip.

The next morning I returned to the PRS department office. A man dressed in slacks and a short sleeve shirt was standing just inside. Rita was away from her desk.

"Hi," I said.

The man eyed me for a moment. I was clean-shaven and, unlike most of the other professors at the college, I was dressed in a sport coat and tie. The man must have figured that I was somebody important. "Hello," he replied at last, smiling. "I'm Royse Smith, professor of political science." He said this in a voice full of pride, as if he were announcing that he was a recipient of the Congressional Medal of Honor. He extended his hand.

"Glad to meet you," I said, grabbing hold of his hand and shaking it warmly. "I'm Lee Miller. I was just hired to teach economics part-time, but my degree is actually in political science."

"Oh, I see," said Professor Smith in a voice tinged with contempt. He pulled his hand away and disappeared into his office.

"Pompous ass," I thought. I was too polite to articulate the words, and I certainly did not want to ruin my chances of getting a full-time job sometime down the line.

A moment later Rita walked in the door. I introduced myself to her, picked up a copy of the textbook for the classes I would teach, signed some forms, and went home. I left as quickly as possible. After the icy reception that Royse Smith had given me, I didn't feel much like talking to anyone else.

I had just five days to get ready for my first class, and I didn't feel very prepared. I had taught macroeconomics only once before, but I had used a different textbook. So over the next five days, I spent every spare moment preparing.

On Monday, I got into my car, eager to begin my first day of work. I turned the key in the ignition. The engine groaned a couple of times and fell silent. It would not start. I tried a second time, with the same result. "Not on my first day!" I moaned. I got a neighbor to jump-start the car, and I drove to Pep Boys to have my battery tested. They were very busy, and kept me waiting for a long time. I didn't have the option to go elsewhere, because I had turned off the ignition and the car would not start again. I felt really stupid. I found a pay phone and called the Henderson campus to tell them that I would be late. Then I waited. An hour later, the technician told me that I needed a new battery. While he installed it, I called Henderson again. Heather, the secretary in the Provost's office, told me that she would cancel my class and send the students home. It was not a very good first day. On the other hand, I realized, Heather had been pleasant and under-standing, and my job would be waiting for me the next day.

My second day went much more smoothly, and by the second week, I felt relaxed and confident in the classroom. Given the low salary, I kept my workload to a minimum, assigning multiple-choice exams that could be electronically scored on the Scantron machine. On an average week I probably spent less than fifteen hours on work-related activities, leaving me plenty of free time. I spent that time revising a fantasy novel, entitled *Passage to the Underworld*, which I had been writing on and off since the fifth grade.

Beth and I stayed at first with her sister and brother-in-law, before finding an inexpensive apartment in a working-class neighborhood on the east side of town.

Beth was very busy in her job. She often had to go to meetings and dinners on nights and weekends. Occasionally, she invited me to help out. It was on one such occasion, on October 19, 1997, that I first met U.S. Senator Harry Reid and his wife Landra. That Sunday afternoon, Beth took me to a reception in honor of the Reids, hosted by the Paradise Democratic Club, at the home of University and Community College Regent Shelley Berkley. Berkley was a candidate for Congress. When Beth introduced me to Senator Reid, I made sure to thank him for introducing me to Richard Moore.

I was struck by how accessible politicians were in Nevada. When I had lived in California, I had trouble getting my congressman's office to return my phone calls. At this event, in contrast, I met just about every important Democratic elected official in the state, from the governor on down. It was refreshing to live in a place where politicians actually spoke to people who were neither important community leaders nor big campaign contributors.

I finished revising *Passage to the Underworld* by late November, and sent off query letters to various literary agents and editors. Among them was James Frenkel. I was amazed that I had remembered his name after all these years. When I had finished the previous draft of the novel in 1986 — I had been a high school senior at the time — I had sent it off to various publishers, including Bluejay Books. Mr. Frenkel, who was the publisher of Bluejay Books, had expressed some interest in my novel in a couple of phone conversations. Unfortunately, Bluejay went out of business, and Mr. Frenkel went to work for TOR Books, after which I went off to college and lost touch with him.

I called up TOR Books, and they put me in touch with Mr. Frenkel. He agreed to take another look at my manuscript. By the following spring, most of the agents and editors to whom I had written had sent me back rejection letters. So had Mr. Frenkel. Given that he and I had something of a relationship dating back many years, I decided to e-mail him to ask for a further explanation as to why he had been so encouraging years ago, but had rejected the manuscript now. To my amazement, he sent me back a lengthy message of encouragement and advice:

Dear Lee Miller:

It's quite possible that we were being kinder than we should have been a long time ago.

I don't know. I do know that it's harder to get books published today than it was eleven or twelve years ago, and I have higher standards now than I did then. Your novel PASSAGE TO THE UNDERWORLD is interesting and flawed, and were I you, and serious about being a writer I'd stop trying to revise the first novel you ever wrote, and go about writing other novels, or better yet, short stories.

13

Fussing with one's first novel is a trap many young writers fall into. You learn far more by writing different things than you do by rewriting the same thing over and over again.

If you're serious about writing, you need to let go of this novel for now. If it's worth the effort, you'll do a much better job rewriting it AFTER you've written other things. If you don't believe me, ask published writers, or other editors or agents. It's just true.

I don't know if you really do want to be a writer, or whether you're just wishing and hoping that you can get this first one published and that will push you to other efforts.

It would be an unwise thing to do. For all the merits of the story, it's just not good enough to publish in its current form, and you'll waste a lot of money sending it all around if you keep doing it. But you do have talent, and if you write other things, you're much more likely to hone that talent sufficiently to get to the point of being a capable fantasy writer, than you are likely to do that by rewriting this book even more.

I've edited a lot of first novels, and a lot of second, third, fourth and fifth novels, and I know that a lot of first novels need to be put aside and then returned to after other works are written by the same writer.

I'm sorry if this comes as a terrible shock to you, but this is the best explanation I have for why you have different reactions from me now and years ago.

Good luck with your writing.

Yours,

James Frenkel

I was disappointed, of course. But I had a choice as to which parts of his message to dwell upon. I could dwell upon his rejection of my book, or I could choose to focus on the part where he said, "you do have talent." I chose the latter option. I took his advice and decided to write something else. Back in college I had started working on a prequel to *Passage to the Underworld*. It focused on a young man named Retsamdros who grew up in a shantytown and who went on to found a powerful empire. I had written only three scenes. The first scene was a sort of prologue, in which the child Retsamdros kills a man trying to molest him. In the second scene, Retsamdros, now a young man, gets arrested for resisting the soldiers raiding the shantytown in which he lives. In the third scene, Retsamdros escapes from prison after bribing the jailer with some money he finds hidden in his cell. I decided to use these three scenes as the seeds of a new novel. I told myself that Mr. Frenkel was right, that I was a talented writer, and that my new novel would be great. I went right to work.

My first semester at CCSN went well. The students and I established a great rapport. They loved my "Star Trek" explanation of federal open market operations: "The 'Federation' has its origins in twentieth century America, where we know it as the 'Federal Reserve,' or 'Fed,' for short. It rules the galaxy through its power over the money supply. Here's how they do it. The Fed sells some bonds. Someone buys those bonds, and the money paid to the Fed for the bonds, from our perspective, ceases to exist. It seems to disappear into another dimension. As a result, the money supply shrinks." At the end of the semester, my students had to fill out evaluation forms. They gave me excellent marks.

Unfortunately, my finances were in a precarious state. I had returned from Japan with nearly $10,000 saved. The first $3,300 went to buy a used car, so that I could get to work. Pretty ironic that my entire pre-tax salary for the first semester equaled the cost of my transportation to and from work. Even worse, I had to spend part of my savings each week to meet my miscellaneous living expenses. When the semester came to an end, my finances deteriorated even further. I received no paychecks for January or February, because adjunct faculty receive paychecks neither during winter vacation nor for the first month of the subsequent semester. I began to wonder whether I might have been better off, had I decided to abandon my dream of being a college professor, and opted instead for the comparative financial stability of waiting tables or valeting cars. But whenever I became depressed about this situation, I buried myself in the fantasy world I was creating. Somehow, my own problems seemed to pale in comparison to those of the brave young man trapped in a dark, cold dungeon.

Back in the real world, things finally began to improve in March. My paycheck that month was double my December paycheck, because I finally had started teaching economics at UNLV as well as at CCSN. Imagine being thrilled to receive a monthly paycheck for $1,695! However ridiculous it may seem, this salary meant that, for the first time since I had arrived in Las Vegas, I no longer had to dip into my savings. This was a very good thing, because my savings were nearly exhausted.

I greatly enjoyed teaching, and I often took the time to chat with my students before class or after. I had over 150 students that semester, and they were quite a varied group. They ranged from kids barely out of high school to senior citizens who had gone back to college after they had retired. I had firemen and police officers in my classes. I even had a student who danced with the Rockettes in one of the hotels on the Strip.

At the beginning of my 8:00 a.m. class one Monday at UNLV, I cheerfully asked my students how their weekend had been. One young man said that his weekend had not been very good. He'd had his wisdom teeth extracted. The young man then proceeded to ask me why I always seemed to be so cheerful.

His question reminded me of something I'd read somewhere before: "Every morning when you get up, you have a choice about how you want to approach life that day," I said to the young man. "I choose to be cheerful.

"Let me give you an example," I continued. The other sixty students in the class ceased their chatter and began to listen to our conversation. "In addition to teaching here at UNLV, I also teach out at the community college in Henderson, about seventeen miles down the freeway from where I live. One day a few weeks ago I drove those seventeen miles to Henderson. I exited the freeway and turned onto College Drive. I only had to drive another quarter-mile down the road to the college. But just then my car died. I tried to start it again, but the engine wouldn't turn over. So I put my flashers on, grabbed my books, and marched down the road to the college.

"As soon as I got there I called AAA and asked them to send a tow truck. The secretary in the Provost's office asked me what had happened. 'This is my lucky day,' I replied, smiling.

"'Your car breaks down and today is your lucky day?' She was puzzled. 'What do you mean?'

"'I live seventeen miles from here.' I replied. 'My car could have broken down anywhere along the freeway. It didn't. Instead, it broke down in the perfect place: off the freeway, within walking distance of here. I'm still able to teach my class, and I've been able to arrange for the tow truck to meet me after class. If my car was meant to break down today, it couldn't have been arranged in a more convenient fashion.'

"The secretary's eyes opened wide, and then she smiled. I smiled back and headed for class." So ended my story to the students in my economics class at UNLV.

I scanned the sixty faces in the lecture hall. Despite the early hour, no one seemed to be asleep. Somehow, my story had touched them. Or maybe it wasn't the story at all. In fact, it had all started with a student's observation that I was cheerful.

A wise man once said, "*Who* you are speaks louder to me than anything you can say." I suppose it must be so.

I attended another political event with Beth that spring. On Senator Reid's recommendation, President Clinton had nominated an African American woman for a federal judgeship. Beth took me to a reception honoring the nominee, held at the West Las Vegas Library, in a historically black neighborhood. I helped to serve drinks and to keep the hors d'oeuvres stocked. The senator and the nominee both made speeches at the event. The most memorable part of the evening for me, however, occurred when things were winding down. Senator and Mrs. Reid made their way through the thinning crowd, saying words of good-bye to the various guests. I was at the opposite end of the room, by the table with the drinks and hors d'oeuvres, watching the Reids make their way toward the door. After Senator Reid said good-bye to someone, he turned toward the door, and somehow his eye caught mine. I smiled and waved. He nodded, and continued walking toward the door, away from where I stood. Suddenly, he leaned over and whispered something to his wife. Then the pair turned and started walking back into the room. They walked straight up to me, and the senator extended his hand. "Dr. Miller," he said, "how is your job-hunting going?"

I shook his hand. "Thanks for asking, senator. I've applied for dozens of full-time professor jobs. Hopefully one of them has my name on it. In the meantime, I'm teaching economics part-time at CCSN and UNLV. Thanks again for introducing me to Dr. Moore."

The senator smiled. "Glad to help," he replied. Then he turned. The senator and his wife walked out the door.

I was thrilled that a U.S. senator would walk all the way across the room just to ask me how my job search was going. What an honor! It really meant a lot to me.

II

How I Got the Job

In the spring of 1998, CCSN finally advertised a full-time position in political science. I applied for the opening, hoping that my year of teaching for peanuts would inspire the search committee to look more favorably upon me, as Charles Okeke had suggested the previous August. I mentioned to my students at CCSN that I had applied for a full-time position, and that I'd appreciate it if anyone who cared to do so would put in a good word for me with the administration. It turns out that quite a few of my students wrote letters to Richard Moore praising me. Most wrote letters without telling me that they had done so, but in many cases, I found out at a later date.

There was one student who made it a point to give me a copy of her letter to Moore after class one day. Kathy was a bright student, several years older than I was. She handed me the letter, and I thanked her. I glanced down at it and noticed that it was typed on letterhead. It was signed, Kathy Von Tobel, Member, Nevada State Assembly.

I'd had no idea that one of my students was a member of the state legislature. The Nevada state legislature, like those of several other western states, meets only every other year. The legislature was not in session in 1998, and Kathy was spending her free time working on a college degree.

I finished off the semester, and again I got great evaluations. Most of the comments were pretty standard, such as "he did a good job explaining the course material and making sure that we understood it" or "he was genuinely concerned about his students." My favorite comment, however, was the following: "He is a very attractive instructor, which made me pay attention, but I usually got confused on whatever he was explaining."

I got hired to teach only one summer course at CCSN during June 1998. Despite my pleas, Rita told me that the PRS department could offer me only this single course. Bernie said that he had no summer courses to offer me at UNLV. The CCSN course was crammed into four weeks, rather than the usual fourteen. The good thing about this arrangement was that I would get paid for the whole semester in one paycheck, rather than having my meager wages spread out over four months. The bad thing was that I would be paid only for one class during the summer term, rather than four, as in the spring semester. In other words, I would earn my normal salary during June, but would receive no income for the three months that followed.

I didn't have much time to worry about this, though. In addition to my accelerated workload, I was scheduled to interview Friday, June 26, for the full-time political science job at CCSN. I spent a lot of time preparing the sample lecture that was part of the interviewing process.

The preparation paid off. On June 26, I dazzled the committee with my insights into the federal campaign finance system in the U.S.

"Let's say you want to run for Congress. What sorts of things might make you a strong candidate?"

The members of the search committee raised their hands, offering such suggestions as charisma, new ideas, and money. I zeroed in on the latter.

"How much money do you think you need to run for Congress? A lot! The average winner in a House race in 1996 spent $669,000, and the average winner in a Senate race spent $4.5 million."

I paused for emphasis. "Pretty expensive, isn't it?" The CCSN professors making up the search committee nodded their heads. "The truth is," I continued, "that the cost of running for Congress has risen by 73% since the 1992 election — just four years earlier.

"So, you want to run for Congress. Where are you going to get the money from? How many of you have a spare $700,000 lying around?"

They laughed.

"So, who are you going to get the money from?" The professors suggested rich donors, corporations, and labor unions.

"So, let's say you find some individuals, corporations, and/or unions with deep pockets to bankroll your campaign. And the voters elect you. Now, you've got a difficult decision to make. Whose interests do you represent now? Do you look out for the interests of the voters who elected you — predominantly poor and middle class — or the interests of the rich elite and corporations who provided most of the money for your campaign?"

I scanned the faces in the room. They were watching me closely. I continued. "Some observers do not consider our political system a democracy, but instead, a plutocracy hidden behind a veneer of democratic elections."

I went on to talk about the campaign finance reforms enacted in the wake of the Watergate scandals, as well as the enormous loopholes in the laws, such as "soft money" and "issue advocacy ads." I could see by the looks on their faces that I had the job in the bag. They asked me a couple of questions, and then asked me to wait outside for a few minutes. I did not have to wait long. Professor Larry Tomlinson, the search committee chair, came out and told me that the committee was very impressed with my interview, and that they would like me to meet with Dr. Silverman, the vice president of CCSN, later that afternoon. Silverman would make the final decision between one other candidate and me. Something in Tomlinson's face told me that this was only a formality. I was thrilled.

I went home for a few hours, and then returned to the office where, the previous August, Richard Moore had left me to wait for "Bob." This time, fortunately, I did not have to wait. JoAnn, Silverman's secretary, ushered me right in. Inside the inner office I met Candace Kant, president-elect of the Faculty Senate, who was there to participate in the final interview. Professor Kant was a woman in her forties, a history professor. She mentioned that the Senate leadership often comes from the PRS department. The prior president (Royse Smith), the current president (Al Balboni), and she, were all from the PRS department.

Bob Silverman arrived after a few moments. He remarked on the fact that I had done my graduate work at UCLA. I noted the fact that

20

he did not seem to remember me from our previous meeting. Just as he was about to ask me a question, the door burst open and Richard Moore rushed in.

"I was thinking about going to the movies this weekend," announced Moore. "Bob, did you hear anything about that new flick with DeNiro and Hoffman?"

"Oh, is that the one called 'Wag the Dog'?" replied Silverman. "I heard it was pretty good."

I nearly fell off my chair. I could not believe that President Moore would barge into a job interview to ask advice on what movie to see over the weekend. I was even more surprised when Silverman and he proceeded to discuss the matter for the next fifteen minutes, ignoring the fact that Professor Kant and I were sitting just a few feet away, waiting to resume the interview.

Finally, Moore left, and Silverman picked up the interview where he had left off, making no mention whatsoever about what had just transpired. He asked me a couple of standard questions, like "How do you see the role of a community college instructor?" and "Where do you see yourself in five years?" Despite being a bit unsettled by Moore's interruption, I gave him my stock answers to the questions. Then he asked me if I had any questions for him.

"Just one," I said. "I really appreciate you taking the time to meet with me. I wonder how soon I can expect to hear back from you about your decision."

Silverman answered without hesitation: "Three or four days," he said. "I just have to decide between you and one other candidate for this position."

I nodded. "Thanks again. It was a pleasure meeting you." I shook Silverman's hand, then Professor Kant's, and departed.

Three days went by. Then four. Then five. I called Silverman's office, and JoAnn took a message. No one called me back. I waited two more days, and called again. JoAnn took another message.

I received my final paycheck from CCSN. I called up Rita to check whether, somehow, a course at CCSN had opened up for me to teach. She said no, nothing until fall semester, at the earliest. My savings were gone, and my paycheck would be just enough to last me for one month, not the three months that I would have to wait for my next paycheck from CCSN. I chewed on my nails and prayed for a miracle. Then I remembered the old adage that God helps those who help themselves, and I drove out to the unemployment office.

I filled out some forms, and stood in line for an hour. When I finally reached the clerk, he told me the following: "We'll process your forms. But it's unlikely that you'll receive any benefits."

"Why?" I asked, incredulous.

"You're a college professor. The law doesn't permit you to claim benefits in the summer time."

"That's not fair," I protested, "They barely pay me enough to live from one paycheck to the next during the rest of the year!"

"I don't make the law," replied the clerk dismissively. "You'll receive a response in the mail." He looked past me. "Next."

I spent the weekend worrying about the future. On Monday, ten days after my interview, I still had not heard anything. I called up Larry Tomlinson, the search committee chair. "I had the impression that the interview with Dr. Silverman went well," I explained. "He told me that he'd get back to me in three or four days. It's been ten days. I've tried calling twice. I've left two messages with his secretary, but no one ever calls me back."

There was a pause at the other end of the line. "I don't understand this," Tomlinson mumbled at last. "I'm going to have to check into this," he replied, "and I'll get back to you tomorrow."

The next day I heard back from neither Silverman nor Tomlinson. On the following day, a full twelve days after my interview, I called Tomlinson again.

"I'm sorry," Tomlinson said to me, "but I just can't find out anything about this. It makes no sense. Just between you and me, when the committee forwarded their recommendation to Dr. Silverman, our recommendation was unanimous in favor of hiring you. I can't imagine what could be causing this delay."

I thanked him for his support and hung up, bewildered and frustrated. "What can I do?" I wondered. Just as I began to sink into despair, I got an idea. I picked up the phone again and called Beth at work. I explained the situation, and asked her if she would ask Senator Reid to call Silverman on my behalf. She said that she would mention it to the senator. Then I called Kathy Von Tobel. She agreed to call on my behalf.

The wait was agonizing. I could not concentrate on my writing, and my sleep was restless that night. I wanted to continue working as a college professor, but teaching part-time had nearly bankrupted me. I really needed this job.

The following afternoon the phone rang. It was Kathy. "I called up Silverman today," she said, "and told him that you are a great teacher and that I hope they'll hire you for the full-time opening. You won't believe how he responded. 'All right already,' he said. 'Senator Reid just called a little while ago. All right already, I'll hire the guy.'"

Kathy could not explain why Silverman had been so reluctant to hire me, despite the search committee's unanimous recommendation that he do so. This puzzled me. But after a few weeks, I stopped thinking about it. I did not learn the ugly truth until nearly a year later.

The next day I received a phone call from Thomas Brown, associate vice president for human resources at CCSN. He offered me the job. I, of course, accepted.

"By the way," I asked, "when will my first paycheck be?"

"The end of September."

"Oh," I said, concerned. "I, uh, just received my final paycheck for my summer teaching, and the end of September is nearly three months away. I applied for unemployment benefits, but the clerk told me that the law doesn't permit teachers to claim benefits during the summer. Is there any way I can get an advance on my first paycheck, to tide me over until the end of September?"

Brown sighed. "No, I'm afraid not. The best I can suggest to you is to get a loan from the Silver State Schools Federal Credit Union. CCSN faculty are eligible for membership. As soon as you receive a letter from me formally offering you the job, take it down to the credit union and apply for a loan."

"Thanks," I said, disappointed. It seemed terribly unfair that I would have to take out a bank loan to meet my expenses. I was broke because I'd had to work at CCSN for nearly a year for practically nothing before I could get a full-time job there.

A few days later, on July 17, I received the letter formally offering me the job. I wrote back accepting the job, and went down to the campus to fill out the paperwork.

Ten days later, I received a form letter from the Nevada Department of Employment. It stated that my unemployment claim had been denied under the provisions of NRS 612.434.

"What's that?" I wondered.

There was a second piece of paper enclosed with the form letter. At the top, in bold red letters, was printed, "Nevada Unemployment Insurance Law." It was divided into dozens of paragraphs, each labeled "NRS 612," followed by a decimal point and three additional digits. NRS, I later found out, stood for Nevada Revised Statutes.

I located NRS 612.434. It read as follows:

> Benefits based on service in an instructional, research, or principal administrative capacity in any educational institution or based on other service in any educational institution must be denied for any period between two successive academic years, or between two regular terms, or paid leave, if that person performs the service in the first of such academic years or terms and there is reasonable assurance of employment in the next academic year or term.

"Crystal clear!" I muttered to myself sarcastically. I read through the paragraph three more times, but the meaning of the paragraph remained murky. The best explanation that I could come up with was what the clerk in the unemployment office had told me: that teachers can't collect unemployment benefits during the summer.

"This is bullshit!" I exclaimed to no one in particular. I was alone in my apartment. "It's absurd and unfair!"

I did what comes naturally to me when I become indignant. I booted up my computer and began writing. I drafted a letter to the editor of the *Las Vegas Review-Journal*. It read as follows:

> To the editor:
>
> Do you think that $12,285 per year is more than enough money to live on? Apparently, the state of Nevada thinks so.
>
> I am an educator. Since last September, I have taught economics to over 200 southern Nevadans. As an adjunct instructor at UNLV and the Community College of Southern Nevada, I have earned the princely wage of $1,950 per three-month class (UNLV) and $1,695 per three-month class (CCSN). Each institution has been careful not to offer me more than 2 classes per semester to teach, lest they be required by law to provide me with benefits, in addition to this excessive salary.

Now, it being summertime, despite my desperate pleas for classes to teach, I have found myself unemployed. As you can imagine, my earnings over the past ten months have not allowed me to save any money. Thus, I realized that, for the first time in my life, I would have to apply for unemployment insurance payments.

There is one problem: as an educator, I am ineligible for unemployment during the summer months. The state's logic is that most educators have traditionally been unemployed during summer months, and that they accordingly get paid salaries substantial enough to get them through the summer.

So much for theory. In practice, it means that underpaid adjunct instructors don't get to eat during the summer months. We are barely paid subsistence wages during the academic year, and then are laid off without the possibility of unemployment insurance payments during the summer.

The state unemployment insurance law is mean-spirited. The state of Nevada should not penalize people solely because they wish to devote their lives to educating their fellow Nevadans.

Lee R. Miller, Ph.D.
Las Vegas

I mailed the letter, and sent copies to my state assemblyman, to another state assemblyman whom I knew, and to Kathy Von Tobel. I felt much better.

I took another look at the letter from the Department of Employment. It indicated that I had the right to submit a letter appealing the decision. I sat down again before my computer and did just that. It began as follows:

I am writing to appeal the determination that I am ineligible for unemployment insurance benefits under section 612.434 of the Nevada unemployment insurance law. I believe that this section of the law was meant only to apply to full-time salaried employees of educational institutions, and cannot reasonably be construed to apply to part-time adjunct employees like myself.

I elaborated on this point, using the arguments that I had articulated in my letter to the editor, although I modified the prose to make it more formal and dignified. I closed my appeal with the following words:

Adjunct instructors are exactly the sort of people that the unemployment insurance system was set up to help. Section 612.434 cannot reasonably be construed to apply to adjunct instructors, and must be construed to apply only

25

to full-time salaried employees. Any other interpretation of this section would go against the spirit of the law, namely, to help people to meet their expenses during temporary involuntary periods of unemployment.

It took just five days for me to receive a response. The Department of Employment notified me in writing that they had scheduled a hearing for my appeal on August 11, 1998. I had ten days to prepare my case.

I called the PRS department. Rita, the department secretary, answered.

"Congratulations on your new job," she said.

"Thanks," I replied. "I'm really excited about it."

We chatted for a few minutes, and then I changed the subject. "Rita, I wonder whether you can do me a favor." I told her about my appeal. "I'm going to have to attend a hearing where they consider my appeal. I'd like to find some people to testify on my behalf. Do you think you could give me the names of some other adjuncts? You know, people like me who don't have another job, who make all their money from teaching. People who are in the same boat as I am."

"Hmm…" replied Rita. "Let me think a minute."

Rita went through the roster of adjuncts teaching in the PRS department. She gave me the names and phone numbers of six people who had no jobs other than working as adjunct college instructors.

I figured that all six would be eager to help me remedy this wrong. After all, if I won, it might establish a precedent that would enable them to collect unemployment benefits as well. I dialed the first number, feeling eager and empowered. I had just begun explaining the situation, when my fellow adjunct interrupted, saying, "I don't want to get involved." Then he hung up on me.

I was crestfallen. I called the next person on the list, and received a similar response. My spirits sank with each rejection. "How could they be so apathetic?" I wondered. "This won't benefit just me—it'll help them as well. I can't understand it!"

The last person on the list was a man whom I will call John, a political science adjunct like myself. I dialed the number, and explained the situation in halting tones, bracing myself for the final rejection.

"Sure," he said. "I'd be glad to help you. What can I do?"

My faith was restored in humanity, and in the virtue of political science instructors.

I asked John to say a few words in support of my position at the hearing. John agreed to do so. He gave me his address, and I mailed him a copy of my appeal, along with a reminder of the time and location of the hearing.

Now I had a witness to testify on my behalf, but I still had to prepare my case. Kathy Von Tobel came to the rescue. She was the only legislator who responded to my letter. She called me up and told me that she agreed entirely with my position, and asked me if there was anything that she could do to help.

"Thanks," I said. "I've got to prepare some arguments for the appeals hearing. Do you think you could get me some background information on the unemployment law?"

"I'll have it faxed down from Carson City right away," she replied. Carson City is the capital of the state of Nevada. Within a couple of days I had a copy of the minutes from the legislative committee hearings on the current law, which took place back in 1977. I spent hours poring over the minutes, preparing my case.

On the morning of August 3, I got a call from Beth. She rarely called me from the office. One of her duties was to go through the morning newspaper and cut out articles that either mentioned Senator Reid or otherwise might be of interest to him. She and the senator's other staff took turns with this task. August 3 was Beth's day.

"Your letter!" she exclaimed. "It's in today's newspaper!"

And so it was. This good news lifted my spirits. I felt that my campaign was gaining momentum.

On the morning of August 11, I arrived at the unemployment appeals office wearing a business suit and carrying a briefcase containing documents in support of my arguments. John was not there. After a short wait, the employment lawyer assigned as the referee for my case called me. I asked the receptionist to send John in as soon as he arrived.

The lawyer was a smartly dressed woman in her early thirties. She led me to a small conference room containing a table, some chairs, and a tape recorder. No one besides the two of us was present. This surprised me. Under Nevada law, the former employer pays the cost of the unemployment benefits. I had expected CCSN to send someone to challenge my appeal.

"Before we begin, before I turn on the tape recorder," said the lawyer, "I just want to tell you something off the record. I was very impressed with your written appeal. That was the most well-written and well-argued appeal I've ever read. It focused clearly on legal arguments, rather than just venting your emotions, like most do. I'm going to keep a copy of it as an example of how an appeal should be written."

"Thank you," I replied, blushing.

She smiled. "By the way, I read your letter to the editor in the *Review-Journal*. It was great."

"Thanks," I said. I was thrilled. "It sounds like she's already on my side," I thought excitedly.

Then the lawyer turned on the tape recorder and asked me for my statement.

"I have a written statement," I said, reaching into my briefcase.

"For the purpose of these proceedings, you will need to read your statement aloud," she said.

"Sure," I replied.

I read my statement. I began by reading the relevant portion of the current statute. I also read the preamble to the first Nevada unemployment insurance law, which was adopted in 1937:

Economic insecurity due to unemployment is a serious menace to the health, welfare, and morals of the people of this state. Involuntary unemployment ... requires appropriate action by the legislature to prevent its spread and to lighten its burden which now so often falls with crushing force upon the unemployed worker and his family.... The legislature therefore declares that ... the public good and well-being of the wage earners of this state require the enactment of this measure ... for the benefit of persons unemployed through no fault of their own.

Denying benefits to adjunct instructors, I contended, violates the spirit of the law, as embodied in this preamble. I went on to reiterate the points that I had made in my letter of appeal, with all the eloquence that I could muster. I quoted court rulings and attorney general's opinions in support of my position.

I also introduced a new argument that I had developed after reading the documents that Kathy had provided me: "The law states that instructors can be denied unemployment benefits for the period between 'two successive academic years' or between 'two regular terms' if the instructor has a 'reasonable assurance' that he or she will resume working during the next year or term. In this case, my period of unemployment falls neither between academic years nor between academic terms. It's right in the middle of the summer term."

The lawyer's ears seemed to perk up. I took a deep breath, and continued. "The state legislature did not define what they meant by a 'regular' term, so we must assume that they used the word 'regular' in the customary fashion. Webster's *9th New Collegiate Dictionary* defines regular as, 'constituted, conducted, or done in conformity with established or prescribed usages, rules, or discipline.'"

The lawyer nodded, and I smiled. "The summer term at CCSN is indeed conducted in conformity with the same federal, state, county, and college rules as are the fall and spring terms," I said. "It is not an academic term that occurs at 'irregular' intervals, but instead it takes place every year." I reached for my briefcase.

"Moreover," I continued, "during the summer term, the same classes are offered as during the spring and fall terms. I worked for the first four weeks of the twelve-week summer term. Hundreds of other instructors also worked during that same summer term. In fact, during the summer term at CCSN there were a total of twenty-five courses offered in economics and political science, the subjects that I teach." I reached inside my briefcase and pulled out the schedules of classes for the fall, spring, and summer terms at CCSN.

"There is absolutely nothing irregular about the summer term," I said. "The fact of the matter is that I was laid off in the middle of the summer term, not between terms."

I handed the lawyer the schedules. "Let the record state," she said, "that the plaintiff has presented to the tribunal copies of the schedule of classes for CCSN, as evidence in support of his contention that the summer term is a 'regular' academic term."

I nodded and continued: "Based on the normal and customary definition of the word 'regular,' the summer term at CCSN is most certainly a 'regular' term. CCSN instructors who are unemployed during the summer are unemployed *during* a regular term, not

29

between regular terms. Therefore, such instructors are *not* ineligible for unemployment benefits just because they find themselves unemployed during the summer."

After I finished my statement, the lawyer asked me a few questions, and then declared the proceedings ended. She turned off the tape recorder. "You did a great job," she said. "I don't suppose you'd consider a change of careers? You'd make a fantastic lawyer."

I laughed. "If things don't work out in my academic career, I'll have to give it some thought."

As I left, I asked the receptionist if John had come in looking for me. She said that he had not. John never called me to explain why he had not shown up as promised. When our paths finally crossed some six months later, he had completely forgotten about ever having spoken with me previously.

III

General Patton and the Three Tenors

A few days later, I had to go to CCSN to fill out some forms and pick up my books for the next semester. When I entered the Department office, I noticed that someone had tacked my letter to the editor to the bulletin board. Rita introduced me to the faculty members present at that time. Each of them, in turn, told me that s/he was surprised that I had written the letter.

"I never would have had the courage to do that, if it had been me that they were considering for a job here," remarked Jim Fuller, a history instructor. "At least not until after I got tenure."

The comment surprised me. "I'm not afraid to point out injustice," I said. I probably sounded a bit too haughty, but I was passionate about this issue. "I couldn't live with myself if I didn't. If this is the sort of place where they hold things like this against you, then it's not the sort of place where I want to work." At the time, I had no idea how prophetic these words would turn out to be.

A few days later I learned that I had won my appeal. I received unemployment checks on a weekly basis until I started working full-time. The benefits were meager, but enough to get me through the summer without having to take out a loan.

Despite the icy reception I had received from Royse Smith a year earlier, the faculty in the PRS department turned out to be very friendly to me. Hopefully, this was unrelated to the fact that Smith was on sabbatical.

A few hours after I had received the call from Thomas Brown offering me the job, Rita had called, giving me the home phone numbers of Charles Okeke and Alan Balboni. Al was a political science professor, as well as the chair of the faculty senate. Rita said he wished to speak to me about teaching a distance education course.

I promised Rita that I'd call them, and hung up the phone. I had scarcely taken my fingers off the handset when the phone rang again. "Hello, is this Lee Miller?" asked a slightly nasal voice.

"Yes," I replied.

"Glad I caught you. My name is Mike Green. I'm a history instructor at CCSN. I'm calling to welcome you aboard."

I was familiar with Mike Green's witty political and historical commentary in *Las Vegas City Life*, a local tabloid, and *Las Vegas Life*, a magazine. Mike was just as amusing on the phone as he was in print. He kept me laughing for an hour with his stories about local politicians and campus personalities.

I told him about my initial contacts with Moore and Silverman. I also mentioned how Silverman had dragged his feet on hiring me until Harry Reid and Kathy Von Tobel had called him on my behalf.

"You know, Moore is very impressed by titles, and Silverman doesn't even go to the bathroom until Moore tells him to. A while back, Moore got Senator Reid to address a meeting of the faculty and staff at the start of the semester. Moore explained excitedly to someone that one of the things he loved about Nevada was that the politicians here are very accessible. 'Take Senator Reid, for example,' he said. 'I had breakfast with him this morning. A U.S. senator! That never would have happened if I was still in California.' I had to laugh," said Mike. "I was very tempted to walk up to Reid and say, 'Hello Senator.' He invariably would have replied, 'Hello Mike.' They all remember names around here. It would have driven Moore up the wall. But I held my tongue."

I laughed. "I'm really glad I got this job. I went through most of my savings working for peanuts as an adjunct, waiting for this position to open up. Charles Okeke had told me back in the fall that if I worked as an adjunct for a while, it would increase my chances of getting hired full-time."

"I'm surprised you understood him when he told you that," replied Mike. "You know, when they hired the new department secretary to work alongside Rita, Charles introduced her to me as 'Venice.' I thought that this girl's parents couldn't possibly have named her after a city in Italy, so for the longest time I avoided using her name. Eventually, I realized that her name was Venus, which sounds like 'Venice' when Charles says it."

I laughed. "I had a lot of trouble understanding him too. How do you find him as a department chair?"

"Charles is a good administrator," replied Mike. "He usually will stand up for us. But it's not easy for him. The pressure from above — and there's plenty of that — tends to wear him down. Charles is a nice guy — too nice, probably, to deal with the people above him."

I nodded. "I guess I'd better try to avoid getting into fights with the administration."

"That's probably a good strategy. But sometimes it's unavoidable."

"Uh-huh," I said, not quite sure why it might be unavoidable. I changed the subject. "Rita asked me to call Dr. Balboni. Something about teaching distance education."

"Oh, so they have you teaching distance ed too. I'm the distance ed guy in history. It's funny. Every so often people come up to me and say, 'Hey, I saw you on TV the other night. It was 3:00 a.m. and I couldn't sleep. I turned on PBS and there you were. I watched you for a while and then I had no trouble falling asleep.'"

I laughed. "With fans like these...."

"Yeah, yeah," said Mike. "PBS broadcasts the lectures for our distance ed courses in the wee hours of the morning. Anyway, the funny thing is, one time I got back an exam from one of my distance ed students. She turned it in to me at a face-to-face class meeting I had scheduled. We usually have a couple of face-to-face meetings, and she had missed the first one. 'You know,' she told me, 'you don't look at all in person like you look on TV. You look so much younger.' I smiled and thanked her for the compliment. When I got home, I noticed that her essays weren't on the topics I had assigned. Sometimes this happens. The students don't know how to answer the questions you give them, so they write about whatever they can think of. But the funny thing is, this student wasn't even writing about U.S. history. She wrote an essay about police stop and frisk procedures, and Miranda rights. I couldn't figure out how she could have written on this topic for my class. Then, suddenly, I remembered what she said to me. 'You don't look at all in person like you look on TV....' I realized what had happened. Somehow, this girl had watched Al Balboni for the whole semester without realizing that it was the wrong class. I don't know how she'd managed this. Maybe the clock for her VCR was slow, and when she taped the lectures, it cut off the beginning part, where they give the title of the course. Although you'd think she'd have figured it out from the subject matter. Anyway, somehow, this girl hadn't figured it out."

I laughed. "Amazing!"

"Balboni is a good guy at heart, but he's kind of our Godfather figure. Maybe it stems from his interest in organized crime. You know he wrote a book about Italians in Las Vegas? Anyway, he likes to see himself as the guy who works behind the scenes, the sort of guy whom everyone respects and goes to for advice. He was pretty surprised when he barely got elected Faculty Senate chair. He makes the right noises about standing up for the interests of faculty before the administration. But a lot of faculty members weren't so sure he'd stand up for them as much as he should. When an administrator says something to me, I start from the assumption that the guy is lying. But Al is a former administrator. When an administrator says something to him, Al tends to start from the assumption that the administrator is telling the truth."

I nodded. "You seem to know a lot about everyone. I guess you have spies everywhere."

Mike laughed. "No, I have no spies. I used to be a journalist, before I was a college instructor. I like to know what's going on, if only to protect myself. I try not to take sides, so I get to hear a little more. You should stay on the sidelines too. That's the best advice I could give you."

"Thanks," I said, not quite sure what he meant. "I'm just going to focus on my teaching and avoid campus politics."

"That's a good idea. But they'll try to rope you into doing some committee work. Try to avoid it as much as possible. A committee keeps minutes and wastes hours. You've got to do it to get tenure, but shop around and volunteer for the committees that meet the least often. My hero is Gary Elliott. He's a history professor in the

34

department. He's a former DEA agent, and he won't take shit from anyone. This year he's on sabbatical, so you probably won't meet him for a while. Anyway, he's notorious for never getting involved in anything. In fact, he lives in California, and arranges his classes so that he can get them all over with in just three or four days per week. He drives into Vegas, gets his teaching over with, and then leaves town again. He never goes to any committee meetings, or even department meetings. As soon as I get tenure, I'm going to stand up at the beginning of the next department meeting and say, 'in the spirit of my hero Gary Elliott, now that I have tenure, I'm out of here.' Then I'll leave, never to attend another meeting."

Mike went on about the people I would meet. He was absolutely charming, and he turned out to be a great friend. He was just about the only person who stood by me when the going got rough. But I'm getting ahead of myself.

Next I called Charles Okeke. He kindly welcomed me to the Department. Then I called Dr. Balboni.

"I'm very pleased to have you on board, Lee," he said in a warm—if rather formal—tone of voice. "You can call me Al." He had a thick accent reminiscent of those I'd heard during my undergraduate days in Boston.

"Thanks. I'm really glad, too," I replied. "Rita said you were the person responsible for distance education classes, and that you wanted to discuss some things with me."

"Well, I wouldn't exactly say I'm 'responsible' for distance ed," said Al. "That's Brad Bleck. But it was I who developed the distance ed program in political science. I produced the videos that we use. I have been teaching the classes. One of the reasons we hired you was to take on some of the burden of the distance ed classes."

"Uh-huh," I said noncommittally. I could see some possible problems on the horizon in taking over a program that someone else had developed. But I tried to keep an open mind. In any case, I was too glad to have finally gotten the job to have many misgivings.

"Well, Lee, I'd like to meet you for lunch sometime soon, so that we can go over some things. I'll bring you copies of my videos."

"I look forward to meeting you in person, Al," I replied.

We arranged to meet a few days later at an Italian restaurant on the fashionable west side of town, near where Al lived. I found him waiting for me at a table outside. He stood and shook my hand. "It's a pleasure to meet you, Lee." He was a middle-aged man with a mustache and large wire-rimmed glasses. Gray hair was combed over to camouflage the bald spot on his scalp. "I think you'll enjoy this restaurant. The food here is very good," he said with a voice of authority, as if he were an expert on restaurants. His wide waistline seemed to add weight to his opinion.

"I get the impression that you're a man who appreciates a good meal," I said. "So do I."

"Good," he said. "Let's order."

Al asked me some questions about my background. He told me much more about his. He had given up a tenured position at a college in Massachusetts a number of years earlier to accept an administrative post at CCSN. Then, due to some sort of philosophical disagreement with the CCSN president of the day, Al had returned to teaching.

I nodded. "I think it's great that you're a man of convictions," I replied sincerely. "It must have been quite a sacrifice."

"Perhaps," he said with a sigh. "But I do enjoy being in the classroom."

"But don't you miss being in a position of leadership and power?"

Al grinned. "Well, my colleagues have called upon me at various times to provide leadership, and currently I'm chair of the Faculty Senate."

"That's quite an honor."

Al nodded. "I know that it's difficult, your first year, learning the ropes. I want you to know that, if you ever have any questions about anything, or need some advice, don't hesitate to call me."

"Thanks," I said. "That really means a lot to me." I was very pleased that so respected a person as the chair of the Faculty Senate had offered to be my mentor.

In August, during the week before classes began, I attended the new faculty orientation. It was a daylong event that consisted primarily of boring talks by various CCSN administrators. We learned about the demographics of the institution, the financial situation, the college facilities, academic policies and regulations, and a host of other very dry topics. By late afternoon, I was struggling to stay awake.

The very last item on our schedule was a visit to the Gaming Department. "Gaming" — a euphemism that avoids the negative connotation of "gambling" — is the name by which the top industry in the state of Nevada called itself. Working as a dealer in casinos can be quite lucrative. I have been told that dealers on the Strip can earn as much as $80,000 per year. Not surprisingly, casinos are rather selective as to whom they will hire as dealers, and they all require that applicants have a certificate in dealing. The Gaming Department at CCSN offers courses leading to this certificate.

The chair of the Gaming Department gave an interesting talk full of humorous anecdotes from his years working as a dealer. We learned, among other things, that when you tip a dealer, s/he is required by federal regulations immediately to drop the tip into a receptacle. All tips are tallied and divided at the end of the day. This requirement was instituted after the IRS came to recognize that dealers earned a lot more than the meager hourly wages they were reporting on their tax returns.

"Couldn't a dealer just pocket the tip?" I asked.

"If your name is Lance Burton, maybe," he replied. Burton is a Las Vegas magician famous for his mastery of sleight of hand. "But the rest of us would get caught on one of the video cameras watching our every move." It's not just the dealers who are being watched. Cameras watch every inch of a casino twenty-four hours a day. In other words, if you feel an urge to pick your nose or adjust your underwear, make sure you step outside first.

After the chair finished his talk, he gave us a tour of the campus casino. Yes, CCSN had a casino on campus equipped with slot machines and all the table games you would find on the Strip, such as craps, roulette, blackjack, and baccarat. The chair told the new faculty members each to pick a table of their choice. A different gaming professor manned each table, ready to teach us the ins and outs of a particular game. I never had played any of them before.

The professor manning the roulette table launched the ball, and it spun round and round the wheel. It could stop on any number, I realized. The outcome was determined by the interaction of all sorts of unknown factors, like humidity, atmospheric pressure, imperfections on the surface of the ball and the wheel, and of course, the degree of force with which the ball was launched. Sort of like events in my life.

I may launch myself on a particular trajectory, with a clear goal in mind, but factors beyond my control often send me spinning off to a different destination entirely. With these thoughts in mind, I approached the spinning wheel. I had launched myself into this new job, and like the ball on the roulette wheel, I had no idea where I finally would land.

Thus, the final segment of my orientation to life as a tenure-track professor at CCSN was learning how to play roulette. I can't say that I ever put this knowledge to much use. While living in Las Vegas, the only time I visited casinos was to frequent the movie theaters and restaurants located there. I think I may have dropped a quarter or two into a slot machine on a couple of occasions while waiting for my girlfriend to come out of the bathroom. But that was about it. It's not that I found gambling to be morally repugnant. I was more than happy to collect a salary paid for with the proceeds from gaming taxes. No, I didn't gamble because it seemed like a waste of time. After all, if the odds were in favor of the gambler, rather than the casino, the gaming industry would collapse, and Las Vegas would revert to sagebrush and tumbleweeds. As a former economics instructor, whenever I feel like gambling, I am more inclined to gamble on the stock market than the slot machine or the roulette wheel. As a human being, I am even more likely to bet on myself.

In the days following the orientation, CCSN offered a number of classes for faculty members. At Al Balboni's suggestion, I took a series of courses on web page design and using the Internet in my teaching. Al had said that he was too busy and too old to be bothered with such things, but that he hoped that I would integrate the new technologies into my curriculum.

I smiled when he told me this. I had watched his distance education videos — more than twenty hours of them. Minute after agonizing minute I had struggled to stay awake through his monotonous lectures. Over the next year, my distance ed students would frequently send me e-mails complaining about how boring the video lectures were. But I never had the heart to mention this to Al.

Finally, opening day rolled around. On the Friday before the start of classes, President Richard Moore ordered all faculty to assemble in the Horn Theater on the Cheyenne campus. The curtains opened, revealing Moore standing before the backdrop of an enormous

American flag. This reminded me of the famous scene in the film "Patton," in which George C. Scott, playing the controversial American general, makes a speech standing before a similar backdrop.

After a speech exhorting us to be creative and innovative, Moore stepped off of the stage. A huge screen was lowered, and the lights dimmed. "Now, I'm going to introduce the new faculty," said Moore. "When I call your name, stand up for us to see you." Headshots of the new faculty members were projected one-by-one onto the screen. Moore announced the name of each new faculty member and where s/he had received his/her masters and/or Ph.D. Finally, the lights brightened, and I could see that some thirty other people were standing, in addition to me.

"And now," said Moore, "we serenade our new faculty." Operatic music filled the theater. Moore played a video of the Three Tenors.

About an hour after the assembly began, the faculty were excused. I ran into Mike Green on the way out. "I'm glad that's over," I whispered to him.

Mike nodded. "It was even longer last year."

"The Three Tenors, and that General Patton thing," I said, shaking my head.

Mike laughed. "Well, now you know how our president likes to run this college."

I did not have any contact with Moore during that semester. But I did see quite a bit of the other professors in my department. I often consulted with Al Balboni, in particular, on various matters related to my job. He always seemed happy to give me his opinion, as if he relished the image of himself as a sort of father figure, a mentor. I held him in very high esteem.

At one point, Al mentioned to me that at CCSN we didn't get much opportunity to teach courses besides the introductory American government course. He said that it was very hard to get enough students to fill up a classroom for any other course.

I found this perplexing, until I came across a course catalogue for the University of Nevada, Las Vegas (UNLV). CCSN was a feeder school for UNLV. Upon examining the political science offerings, I noticed that virtually all of the introductory political science courses offered at UNLV were designated as third- or fourth-year classes.

"Al," I said, "at UCLA, *introduction* to comparative politics or *introduction* to international relations or *introduction* to political theory — they're all *first*-year courses. At UNLV they're third- and fourth-year courses. No wonder you have trouble convincing students at CCSN to take these courses. They only count as electives at UNLV. They don't count toward a political science major there. This is terribly unfair to the students. Our faculty are at least as well qualified to teach these introductory courses as are the faculty at UNLV, and it costs less than half as much to take a course at CCSN."

Al was very excited about this new insight, and he asked Charles Okeke to arrange a meeting with the political science department chair at UNLV to discuss re-designating the introductory classes as first-year courses. Charles took no action.

I was excited at the prospect of doing something to repay Al for all the help he had given me, and I asked Charles about this issue myself. Our department chair was reluctant to schedule such a meeting, speculating that the classes were numbered that way on purpose, so that UNLV political science majors would continue to fill up classrooms at UNLV, rather than at CCSN. I kept badgering Charles on this issue, and eventually he relented. Charles finally told me that he would arrange this meeting as long as all the political science faculty at CCSN were in unanimous agreement in support of this proposal.

Al congratulated me on finally making some headway, and he urged me to contact all of the political science instructors at CCSN to gauge their support. All were supportive of the idea, except for Royse Smith.

I had not come across Mr. Smith since my brief encounter with him when I was hired to teach economics part-time over a year earlier. During the current 1998–99 academic year, he was on sabbatical, working on his doctorate at the University of Nevada, Reno (UNR).

Al arranged a breakfast meeting between himself, Royse, and me. Royse refused to support the proposal, fearing that it would set a precedent that might upset his professors at UNR. They might be disturbed, Royse explained, by the prospect of community colleges stealing away their students. Royse was concerned that their displeasure might put into jeopardy his chances of being awarded a

Ph.D. Al tried to work out a compromise, but in the end, the proposal died.

That was my first and only attempt to reform anything at CCSN. After this I decided that it was a waste of time, and instead focused my energies on designing interesting courses for my students.

There wasn't space in the Philosophical and Regional Studies (PRS) office suite to accommodate me. My office was out in a trailer in the back of the Cheyenne campus of CCSN. The advantage of this location was that its isolation gave me lots of peace and quiet. The disadvantage was that I didn't have much opportunity to interact with the other PRS faculty on campus. Mike Green and Billy Monkman were exceptions; I interacted with them on a social basis.

I had first encountered Dr. Guillermo Monkman during spring 1998, while I was still teaching economics part-time. Charles Okeke had assigned him to evaluate my teaching. Dr. Monkman gave me a favorable evaluation, which undoubtedly proved helpful when I applied for a full-time job. Indeed, Dr. Monkman was one of the members of the committee that interviewed me, and I later found out that he had been a strong advocate for hiring me.

Billy, as he liked to be called, was a tall man in his thirties with a dark mustache and a receding hairline. He was from Argentina, and told amusing stories about his time serving in the military during the Falkland Islands war with Britain: "I told them, 'You guys are crazy. They're going to kill us!' But they didn't listen to me, and look how things turned out."

Billy, a passionate Argentine leftist, had strong views on just about everything, and never hesitated to tell you exactly what they were. He was a great guy with a big heart, but not the sort of person you could easily talk to. With Billy, you just had to listen.

Billy had a huge house with lots of land on the east side of town, not very far from where I lived. He recently had received tenure, and often would invite junior (untenured) faculty members over for drinks. They were an interesting group, far outside the Nevada conservative political mainstream. In addition to the historian and liberal newspaper columnist Mike Green, there was philosophy instructor Mark Rauls, who sported shoulder-length hair. Historian Jim Fuller's hair was of a more conservative cut, but he always elicited cheers of approval with his diatribes against President Clinton as being "much too right-wing for me." Fuller was a supporter of the Libertarian Party, a small political party known for its extremely liberal positions on issues of social policy, such as advocating the legalization of drugs.

I was touched that they included me in their get-togethers. The first time I was there, I asked in an off-hand way whether they ever got together with the more senior faculty members. Billy mumbled something about the senior faculty members being too busy with their families, and then changed the subject.

What Billy said was technically correct. Most of the faculty who attended these get-togethers had no kids. But there was more to it than this. Like many other departments, PRS suffered from divisions, resentments, and ill feelings.

Part of this was just the normal division that one encounters between senior and junior faculty in any department. But it was more complicated than this. Al Balboni and Candace Kant were senior faculty members, but received a good deal of support at times from junior faculty. Most of the junior faculty members who attended Billy's get-togethers, however, tended to resent the "political games," as they saw it, played by the establishment-oriented professors. At times they seemed to kowtow to the administration, at other times to take it on. They were perceived as playing the game for their own benefit, seeking prizes such as administrative jobs, reduced teaching loads, or at least the feeling that what they said mattered to the higher-ups.

This problem existed throughout the college. When Balboni ran for faculty senate chair, a job he had held before, he did it in part because the front-runner was seen by many as lacking sufficient self-restraint. Balboni seemed likely to win easily, given his reputation and seniority, but ended up winning by only a handful of votes. According to Mike Green, most faculty members voted for the candidate they thought would "do a better job of telling Richard Moore to stick it." The closeness of the vote reflected the fact that many faculty members viewed Balboni as too willing to take at face value what he was told by the administration.

I felt that I was on pretty good terms with everyone in the department, and I tried the best I could to stay out of this feud.

IV

The Ferengi, the Garbage Picker, and the Stripper

I've never thought that lecturing is a very good teaching tool. No matter how good the lecture or the lecturer, you always will find students reading, doing homework for another class, or even nodding off to sleep. As such, I emphasized discussion and debate in my classes. Not only did the students find this interesting and stimulating, but I also learned a lot from listening to them.

A community college is open to the entire community, regardless of age or background. This results in a fascinatingly diverse student body. I have taught students from seventeen to seventy years old. I've heard differing perspectives on Social Security from retired people and young people just entering the workforce. I've heard differing perspectives on mandatory school uniforms from parents, teachers, and recent high school graduates. I've heard first-hand accounts of the Gulf War and the invasion of Panama from veterans. I've learned about running for office from state and local elected officials. I've learned about public administration from county civil servants. I heard very different viewpoints on alleged police brutality and racial profiling from white police officers and African American civilians.

One semester, a group of three students — Kurt Gunther, Dennis Gatbonton, and Joel Jacks — asked me if they could produce a documentary on homelessness. I was impressed by their ambition, but skeptical that they could pull it off. They pleaded with me, and eventually I gave them my blessing. They produced a fascinating series of interviews with residents at MASH Village, a homeless shelter in downtown Las Vegas. A recovering drug addict, as well as a homeless family, told the stories of how they became homeless, how people treated them, and what sort of services were available to help them with their plight. I was so impressed with the video that I showed it to all my classes. I nominated the three student producers for an award. The university and community college Board of Regents honored them, along with several other students, at a banquet that year.

One of the most amusing stories about my students concerned Todd Agnello. I learned over the course of several weeks that Todd was a very bright young man. But what I noticed about him on the very first day of class was that he wore blue nail polish. Every day I noticed the nail polish, and every day I grew more curious. I figured that he might be a cross dresser, but blue did seem to be a rather odd color. I didn't want to embarrass him, however, and refrained from asking. But, finally, after three weeks my curiosity got the better of me.

"Todd," I whispered to him, stroking my fingernails, "why blue?"

"Oh, it's for work," he said, laughing. "I'm a Ferengi at the Star Trek Experience. It's just too much of a hassle to take off the nail polish everyday, so I just leave it on." The Ferengi, in case you don't know, are an avaricious race of aliens often seen on the Star Trek spin-off "Deep Space 9." The Star Trek Experience is an attraction at the Las Vegas Hilton.

The most outstanding student I encountered at CCSN was a man by the name of Norman Schilling. Norm enrolled in one of my night classes in fall 1998. This thirty-something mustached man always sat in the front row, and was never afraid to express his views in class, no matter how controversial they were. He impressed me greatly with his passionate conviction that the government should do more to help the poor and less fortunate members of society. I was very disappointed when he dropped my class after the first couple of weeks.

The following semester, Norm was back. He explained to me that his work schedule during the previous semester had gotten too hectic, forcing him to drop. He said that he had really enjoyed my class, and had made it a point to sign up this semester for a section of American government taught by me, rather than one taught by another professor. I was flattered.

Norm blew me away with a very thoughtful and compelling research paper advocating the legalization of marijuana. The assignment was to write seven pages. Norm wrote thirty pages. It is, of course, easy to ramble on for thirty pages. Norm, however, wrote a well-researched, succinct, and cogent paper.

When he did an oral presentation on the same subject, to my amazement, his oratorical talents swayed several of the most conservative members of the class. I remember seeing heads nodding in agreement when he gave his final argument: "I have a friend who is a hard-working husband and father. He's a good man, someone you can always count on, no matter what. He pays his taxes and generally is a law-abiding citizen, except for one thing. He smokes marijuana recreationally. He doesn't deal drugs, and his habit doesn't intrude on anyone else's life but his own. If the authorities were to find out that he smoked pot, all this would change. He could be thrown in jail. His family would lose their breadwinner and end up on the street. Once he's in jail, he would no longer be a taxpayer, and instead would become a burden on society. So would his family. Why? Not because he uses drugs. No, his drug use has no effect on anyone but himself. No, he and his family would become a burden on society because it is illegal for him to do something that harms no one, except perhaps himself. This makes no sense at all."

Norm easily gained the respect of the other students in the class, and many badgered him to run for Student Government. Eventually he acquiesced. His classmates were disappointed to learn that Norm was ineligible, because he was enrolled in too few classes. Only students taking at least two classes were permitted to serve in the Student Government. Norm's work schedule had permitted him to take only one class that semester.

That did not stop Norm from getting involved in politics. He spearheaded a local campaign for environmental justice. Silver State Disposal, the local garbage monopoly, was trying to convince state regulators to close down Western Elite, a firm that composted construction debris. The compost was later sold for landscaping purposes. Silver State contended that Western Elite was selling too small a percentage of the compost to be classified under the law as a recycler, and therefore was operating an illegal landfill. The controversy came to a head when the Las Vegas city council rejected Western Elite's bid to turn sewage sludge into fertilizer, and instead accepted the higher-priced bid submitted by Silver State to bury the sludge. The city contended that it was contractually obligated to award the contract to Silver State, because it previously had granted that company an exclusive franchise on waste disposal.[1]

I was amazed when I got to know Norm better, and he told me about his background. This great orator and intellectual was a self-made, self-taught man. Norm's oratorical skills came from natural ability, honed by practice talking to people about topics that he cared about. His large vocabulary and vast knowledge came from his love of reading. He even spoke two foreign languages. He was a true Renaissance man.

After graduating from high school, Norm had supported himself by working at various menial jobs: gas station attendant, busing tables at restaurants, and washing dishes. On Saturdays he also would pick through the trash at the dump and sell the items he retrieved at the swap meet the following day. Eventually Norm was offered a job directing traffic at the dump.

While working at the dump, Norm came into daily contact with people hauling grass clippings and other yard waste, sparking his interest in gardening. He opened his own gardening business, and started taking classes at CCSN to increase his knowledge of horticulture.

Eventually, he was hired to be lead groundskeeper with the Water District. He was a visionary who pioneered the transition to low-water desert landscaping in the Las Vegas Valley. Later, he became lead groundskeeper at the Desert Demonstration Gardens, where he worked at encouraging the public to engage in more environmentally-friendly landscaping techniques.

Of course, not all of my students were as outstanding as Norm. In fact, plagiarism seemed to be endemic to my classes. One semester, for example, I received a very well-written paper advocating the legalization of marijuana for medical purposes. It was full of references to various medical studies, and cited high-powered journals like the *New England Journal of Medicine* and *Lancet*. In fact, it looked like something that should be published in one of those journals.

I described the student and my concerns about plagiarism to Al Balboni. He honed in right away on the race of the student. "He's black? You'd better be very careful, or he'll slap you with a discrimination lawsuit," observed my mentor. "Of course, how you handle this is totally up to you. But this is what I would do. I wouldn't accuse him of cheating. I'd just ask him where he got the material for his paper. Tell him that his paper was very well-written, and ask him whether he wrote it all himself, or used someone else's words. Chances are, he'll just admit that he copied the paper from somewhere. If so, it means he probably plagiarized out of ignorance. If he were my student, I would show mercy. Rather than bringing the matter to the attention of the administration, putting a black mark on his academic record, I'd handle this myself. I'd make it clear to the student that what he had done was wrong, and I'd make him re-write the paper in his own words."

I took Al's advice. The student readily admitted that he had copied the paper out of a book. I had him re-write the paper in his own words, and as penance, I assigned him an additional essay on plagiarism.

This was only one of several instances of plagiarism that semester. The next semester, there were more. One was particularly memorable. "I know I've read this somewhere before," I muttered to myself as I finished reading a particularly well-written paper. I looked at the student's name. The author was a bright young woman, whose work was always very good. "Did she show me a draft of this?" I wondered, scratching my head. No, I realized, she had not. I glanced down at the student's name again, and then it hit me.

After class the next day I pulled the young woman aside. "Is Jennifer by any chance your sister?" I casually asked the young woman.

"Yes," she replied.

I sighed. "You're in a lot of trouble."

The young woman's eyes opened wide. "What do you mean?"

I held up the essay. "This paper that you turned in—it is the same one your sister turned in to me last semester. That's plagiarism. You can't copy your sister's work."

47

"But it's *my* work," insisted the young woman. "I was the one who wrote *her* paper last semester."

I shook my head, trying not to laugh. The young woman's punishment for being her sister's ghost writer was to write another essay on a completely different topic, plus, of course, an additional essay on plagiarism. Her work was excellent, and after she had done her penance, I gave her an "A" in the class.

Some of my students were brilliant, and some were dishonest. There was one student, however, who taught me a lot about myself. Actually, she was not one of my students, but she was a full-time student at CCSN. I met her in a ballroom dancing class that I took for fun in fall 1998. I will call her Ai Vi.

Ai Vi had the tiny waist and curvaceous hips common to Southeast Asian women. Atypically, however, she had abundant cleavage. All this I could easily see while I danced with her. I later had the opportunity to get a much closer look.

Ai Vi told me that she was a belly dancer at Caesars·Palace, and that she was taking ballroom dancing because she was interested in learning some new dance styles. She was a wonderful dancer and, without question, the most beautiful woman in the class.

Ai Vi and I became friends. We both loved hiking, and made several trips together to Red Rock Canyon and Mt. Charleston, two scenic areas near Las Vegas.

One day Ai Vi invited me to watch her dance.

"At Caesars?" I asked.

"No, I don't work there anymore. The schedule interfered with my classes. I have a new job."

"Do you dance at a Middle Eastern restaurant?" Recently I had been to a restaurant on Paradise Road that featured belly dancers.

"No, no more belly dancing. It's a different kind of dancing."

"What kind of dancing?" I asked, intrigued by her secrecy.

"You may not like what I tell you. But I want my friends to know the real me. If they don't like me for who I am, then they can go to hell."

"Don't worry about me, Ai Vi. I won't look down on you. What sort of dancing do you do?"

"I'm a stripper at a club downtown."

I indeed was surprised. But I consider myself to be fairly liberal, and I try not to judge people.

"So, will you come and see me today at 4:00? It's better if you come early. If you come at night, I'll be really busy, and I won't be able to talk to you."

I agreed to be at the club at 4 p.m.

I had been to a strip club only once before. That was when I was 18 years old, living in San Diego. My buddies had decided to take our friend Bob to a place called The Body Shop for his eighteenth birthday. It certainly had been an eye-opening experience for me, but not one, up till this point, that I had chosen to repeat.

Downtown Las Vegas does not have the glitz and glamour of the famous Las Vegas Strip. It tends to be downright seedy. The club in question, The Talk of the Town, looked okay from the outside, though. My car was only one of three in the parking lot. Still early, I thought. I was a bit embarrassed getting out of my car, glancing this way and that to see if any pedestrians had me in their line of sight, and then I made a mad dash for the door. That seems sort of silly, now, in retrospect. If my goal was to avoid attracting attention to myself, I probably should have walked. But I doubt that anyone noticed me, quiet as it was at that time of day.

At first, I thought I had entered the wrong door. I found myself amidst row after row of adult videos. I was the only patron, and a man sat behind the counter, looking bored. I was too embarrassed to ask him where the entrance to the club was, and I was just about to leave, when I noticed a nondescript doorway at the back of the video store. "That must be it," I thought, and headed toward it.

Just beyond the doorway sat a bald man on a high stool. "Uh, how much?" I asked nervously.

The man pointed to a hand lettered sign on the wall, which read, "Admission $10." I handed the man a $10 bill. He grunted and gestured for me to come in.

A scantily-clad hostess was waiting for me. "You have to buy a drink," she said, leading me to the bar. I noticed no bottles of liquor. Behind the bar was a sign listing two types of soft drinks and water. "No alcohol?" I asked the hostess.

"What you see is what you get," she replied, gesturing to the sign. I asked for a bottle of water, handing the bartender a $20 bill. He gave me a tiny bottle, and fifteen singles in change.

The showroom was small. The stage was a rectangular platform, perhaps fifteen feet by twenty. It was fairly plain, with no curtain, adorned only by a couple of brass poles running from floor to ceiling. Around the stage were three rows of tiny tables, each with one chair, facing the stage. In the back of the room were some couches.

The hostess seated me at a table abutting the stage. There were just three other men in the audience. Soon, the music began. A woman emerged from a doorway wedged between the bar and the entrance, and climbed up onto the stage. I simultaneously felt the urge to shyly avert my eyes and to stare shamelessly at the woman on stage. The latter impulse won out.

A couple of other acts preceded Ai Vi's. The first stripper was a skinny brunette with no breasts to speak of. The second was an overweight blonde with huge breasts. Then Ai Vi came out. She had the sort of body that men kill each other over: long, shapely legs, curvaceous hips, tight ass, tiny waist, and large firm breasts. I noticed her breasts, in particular — not just because they were among the parts of a woman's anatomy that most fascinated me — but because they were perfectly shaped. On a later occasion, I asked Ai Vi if they were natural. She was not at all embarrassed to tell me that that they were surgically enhanced. She said that, ever since she was a little girl, she had wanted large breasts, even though she had never seen a woman who actually had large breasts. Vietnamese women tend not to have much in the way of cleavage.

Ai Vi danced wonderfully, teasingly, sensuously. Piece by piece she removed each article of clothing, often pausing to give the men in the audience an opportunity to slip dollar bills into her bra or her waistband. This I did several times. When she was totally nude, she approached me. "Put it in your teeth," she whispered. I held the dollar bill between my teeth, as she had ordered. She turned around, so that her back was to me, her buttocks just above eye-level. Then she spread her legs wide, and bent over. The dollar bill just barely touched her pubic hair, and my face nearly did as well. She reached between her legs and grabbed the bill. Then she danced before me for a minute, before moving on to the next table.

I was so aroused that I thought I would explode. I had to keep telling myself that this was just her job. But, wow, was she good at what she did!

After Ai Vi finished her act, she threw a robe around herself and headed for the dressing room. A few minutes later she emerged, fully-clothed, but in a suitably revealing outfit. She led me to one of the sofas at the back of the room.

As soon as we sat down, a barmaid approached. "Do you want to buy the lady a drink?" she said in a tone of voice that was more of an order than a question.

I asked Ai Vi what she wanted. She ordered a Coke. While she sipped it, we sat and talked. The funny thing is, our conversation was like any other conversation that we'd had previously in less unusual locales. We talked about her family, her dogs, her classes, and a host of other topics that had absolutely nothing to do with stripping or with sex. There was a certain irony about it all. It was difficult in my mind to square the image of Ai Vi the intelligent young woman—my friend—with the woman who had earlier presented herself to me and the other men in the audience as nothing but an object of male lust.

This experience dispelled my prejudices against the "sort of women" who make their living as strippers. I saw Ai Vi as a person, not as a mere sex object. She was gorgeous, and very sexy, but she was also very human. I'm glad I got to know her *before* I saw her strip.

Some weeks later, I asked Ai Vi how it is that she had decided to become a stripper. She said that originally, she had done it to get back at a man who had hurt her. She had also modeled nude for some prominent men's magazines. Ai Vi told me that she had tried working other jobs, but that they always took too much time away from her studies. As a stripper, in contrast, she could earn plenty of money working just one or two nights per week.

Ai Vi was not just beautiful, but also very intelligent. She had invested her earnings in the stock market, and had amassed a nice nest egg. She planned to use it, eventually, to finance her graduate studies. Her goal was to get a Ph.D. in psychology.

A year later, Ai Vi was married.

V

Friends in High Places

During fall 1998, Beth and I spent countless hours volunteering for Harry Reid's re-election campaign. We registered people to vote at a bus station. We knocked on doors in a scary-looking neighborhood, and I almost got bitten by an angry dog. We nearly got into a brawl with supporters of Reid's opponent outside a TV station in which the two candidates were holding a televised debate. We even served as delegates at the state Democratic convention. Some activities were boring, some were fun, and some were stressful. I can think of one event that had all three of these characteristics.

The campaign staff had organized a barbecue at Casa de Shenandoah, the home of singer Wayne Newton. Newton's place, in stark contrast to the neighboring single family homes, was a sprawling ranch complete with an enormous house, stables, and lots of lawn space for the barbecue. It was situated on Pecos Road, a busy thoroughfare with four lanes of traffic. Several hundred guests were expected, and it was my job to assist them with parking.

Emmett Clark, a Reid lieutenant brought in from Washington for the final stretch of the campaign, was in charge. He assigned me the task of directing the cars to park on a small side street just beyond the boundaries of the ranch.

At first this job was really boring. I stood around in my Harry Reid tee-shirt, waiting for cars to pull up, shading myself from the hot desert sun in the shadow of a large tree. A car or two arrived every five to ten minutes, and I directed them to drive a bit further down the street. Another volunteer at the side street directed them to park there.

As the afternoon wore on, however, the cars started coming with ever-greater frequency, until they became a steady stream. The traffic began to get backed up along Pecos from the side street to which I was directing it. Suddenly, my partner down the road came running out, waving to me. "Hey, the neighbors are getting ready to lynch us!" he shouted.

I ran down to see what he was talking about. The side street was clogged with traffic. Every available parking space on the ranch side was full. Drivers were attempting to park in front of the houses on the other side of the street. The owners of those houses were out patrolling in their pickup trucks, trying to turn back the traffic.

"Just because Newton is a celebrity," shouted one irate neighbor, "it doesn't mean he owns our street! We're not going to let these people block our driveways!"

There was probably enough space for about twenty cars maximum to park on that small street. "Where are they planning to put the other hundred?" I wondered. "Let's tell them to back out," I told my partner, "and have them park on Pecos."

He nodded, and I ran back out to put the plan into action. At my direction, drivers started parking their cars on the ranch side of Pecos Road. Within another fifteen minutes, all parking spaces along Pecos were full within a quarter mile of the ranch. Drivers started making U-turns and parking on the other side of the street. Crowds of people — including children and the elderly — were now running across four lanes of traffic to get to the entrance to the ranch. I ran to get Emmett.

"There are no spaces left on this side of the street," I gasped. "Someone's gonna get run over crossing with all this traffic."

"Deal with it!" shouted Emmett, turning away to face the line of volunteers and staff members with other pressing problems.

I ran back to the street. I proceeded to stop traffic periodically, and to escort the people across the street. It was a harrowing experience, with lots of angry drivers honking their horns, but the operation proceeded successfully.

Of course, it was too good to last. It didn't take long for all the parking spaces on the other side of the street to fill up. But the cars still kept coming. What was I to do?

I remembered passing a supermarket on Sunset, the street forming the northern boundary of the ranch. I grabbed a magic marker from the guest registration table and pulled a cardboard campaign sign off the wall of the ranch. I turned the sign over, and wrote the following: "Park at Market." Below the words I drew a big arrow pointing left. I ran the quarter mile north to the intersection of Pecos and Sunset. I stood there, holding the sign aloft. The traffic was heavy, and only a few drivers were able to cut across to the left lane to make the turn. The others moved over when they were able, and made U-turns. But, finally, the problem was solved.

By the time the sun was ready to go down, parking spaces were opening up on the ranch side of Pecos. I breathed a sigh of relief and retired my sign. But there was no rest for the weary. The line for food inside the ranch was miles long, and I was drafted to help speed up the distribution. An hour later, the line had disappeared. But so had the food.

As Wayne Newton sang his good-byes, Beth and I slipped away, exhausted and hungry. We stopped off at our favorite Indian restaurant on the way home.

Eventually, Election Day arrived. On the evening of November 3, 1998, Beth and I joined staff and volunteers from the campaigns of various Democratic candidates at the ballroom of the MGM Grand Hotel's Convention Center. The election results for the various races came in one by one. The hour grew later and later, but the results of the U.S. Senate race remained too close to call. By midnight, I was exhausted, and went home. Beth stayed all night. When she got home the next morning at 9:30 a.m., the winner still had not been announced. It turned out that the Elections Department in Washoe County, in northern Nevada, was having trouble counting the absentee ballots. In the end, about 500 absentee ballots had proven to be unreadable by the optical scanner, and Elections Department officials had found it necessary to re-copy the voters' choices onto fresh ballots.

The results from Washoe County did not come in until 9:58 a.m. on Wednesday, November 4, the day after the election. Reid had won by only 459 votes statewide. Not surprisingly, given the irregularities in the ballot counting, three days later a judge ordered a recount of all 15,000 absentee ballots from Washoe County. The following day, Sunday, November 8, elections officials discovered that the printing was misaligned one-sixteenth of an inch on 6,000 Washoe County ballots, rendering them unreadable by the vote counting machines. This forced them to recount these ballots by hand, which was time-consuming. The Washoe County recount was not completed until Thursday, November 12. Reid's margin of victory had shrunk to 401 votes. On Wednesday, November 25, the Nevada Supreme Court certified the election results.

The ordeal, however, was far from over. On November 30, Congressman John Ensign, Reid's opponent, officially demanded a statewide recount. Two days later, he filed a lawsuit demanding a full recount by hand of all ballots from Washoe County. On December 4, a judge rejected Ensign's lawsuit for a recount by hand, but the statewide recount was allowed to continue. On December 9, with the results of the recount announced from all counties besides Washoe, Reid was still ahead by 379 votes. Ensign finally conceded. The following day, the final results were announced. A full 37 days after the election, Reid was finally declared the winner. He had won by only 428 votes statewide. The Democrats breathed a sigh of relief, and soon thereafter Harry Reid assumed the office of Assistant Minority Leader of the U.S. Senate.

In December, Richard Moore held his annual Christmas party at his huge home in a posh neighborhood on the west side of town. He invited all CCSN employees, plus just about every politician and dignitary in the county. Beth told me that Senator Reid had received an invitation, although I never ran into him at the party. I did, however, run into Bob Silverman. To my surprise, he remembered me.

"Lee," he said, calling to me from across the room, where he stood chatting with a couple of people. I approached.

"This is Dr. Lee Miller," announced Vice President Silverman to the people beside him. "He's a friend of Harry Reid."

I found it amusing that Senator Reid's call on my behalf had made such an impression on Bob Silverman. The senator, of course, was more of an acquaintance than a friend. But I figured that it wouldn't hurt me if my boss continued to believe that I had friends in high places, so I did not correct the mistake.

During my first year as a full-time instructor at CCSN, I tried to follow Mike Green's advice to avoid doing anything that might bring down the wrath of the administration. It is true that my classes discussed controversial topics. One book I assigned was a Marxist interpretation of the U.S. political system, arguing that democracy was a sham and that the government served only the interests of big business; another book argued for the legalization of "consensual crimes" such as gambling, prostitution, and drug use. But the students loved our discussions and debates of controversial topics, and no one complained to my supervisors.

I saw my role as more than a mere *teacher* of political science. I tried to cajole and inspire students into becoming more active participants in the political process. I invited many prominent politicians to speak to my students, and when they accepted, I usually reserved a large auditorium and invited the whole campus to attend. During the fall semester, State Assemblywoman Kathy Von Tobel and U.S. Senator Harry Reid accepted my invitation. During the spring semester, County Recorder Judy Vandever, University and Community College Regent Steve Sisolak, and Congresswoman Shelley Berkley came; Kathy Von Tobel also made a return visit. They spoke on diverse topics, ranging from campaigning for public office to U.S. policy toward Yugoslavia. They stayed late, and answered lots of questions.

Steve Sisolak, in particular, inspired my students to get involved in political activities. Steve had made headlines during the winter of 1998–99 by denouncing the funding disparity between northern and southern Nevada colleges, and advocating that the state spend the same amount of money per student in the south as in the north. This issue was not new. The center of power in the state had always been in the north. This disparity had persisted despite the fact that economic and demographic factors had shifted to favor the south more than half a century ago. Two-thirds of the state population and most of its industry were now located in the Las Vegas metropolitan area.

The state capitol, however, remained in the northern town of Carson City. The Nevada state legislature was a body of amateurs, which met for just 120 days every other year, and got paid virtually nothing for their work. As such, those legislators who lived closest to the capitol had a competitive advantage over those who lived far away. The northern legislators could just drive home every night while the legislature was in session, and keep in close contact with their constituents, while the southerners had to sleep in motel rooms and were anxious to finish all business for the legislative session and return to their distant homes.

The Regents had long ignored the funding disparity issue. Steve had made it into his *cause célèbre*. He spoke loudly and passionately in favor of correcting what he deemed to be a great injustice.

I first met him at a Regents meeting being held at the West Charleston campus of CCSN on February 25. Steve grilled UNR President Joe Crowley about the wisdom of spending millions of dollars of public money to found a new community college in a sparsely populated area of northern Nevada, at a time when UNLV and CCSN were, in Steve's opinion, being starved for resources. Crowley stuck to his argument that the population in the vicinity of the proposed college was expected to grow significantly over the next decade. Steve claimed that the party that had offered to donate the land on which to build the proposed college had done so in the expectation of making money, because their adjacent property would increase significantly in value once the state had spent millions of dollars building a college next door. (The party offering to donate the land, of course, claimed that its motivations were purely altruistic.) Steve further argued that it was folly to divert even more resources to the sparsely populated north, in the *expectation* of population growth, when there was *real* and staggering population growth going on at that time in the Las Vegas metropolitan area (in the range of 6,000 newcomers per month).

After the speech, I congratulated Steve on making some very compelling points, and I invited him to address my classes. He accepted, and inspired many students to contact their legislators on this issue. Unfortunately for Steve, however, the legislature only agreed to a cosmetic fix of the problem. This was, according to Steve, the result of horse trading between some powerful legislators from the southern city of Henderson (just outside Las Vegas) and their northern counterparts. Apparently, the southerners had agreed not to correct the funding disparity between northern and southern colleges, and to accept the founding of a new northern college, as long as the northerners agreed to accept the founding of a new state college in Henderson. Regardless of this defeat, I admired Steve greatly, and we developed a friendship.

I worked hard at increasing voter registration among college students. I took a class to get certified as a Field Registrar with the Clark County Elections Department. Then I required all of my students to either register to vote or write me a paragraph on why they chose not to register. I saw this as a great learning exercise for my students. Either they would take the first step toward participating in our political system, or they would have to develop an argument against taking such a step. Given that it took only about two minutes to fill out a voter registration form, virtually all of my students chose to register. I ended up registering several hundred students to vote.

Only once did a student choose to write an explanation as to why he did not want to register. The student, whom I'll call Joe, was a gray-haired man nearly twice my age. In class discussions, he often expressed his deep distrust of the government. Joe wrote me a paragraph about how he thought that voting was a waste of time, and that his vote would have no impact on public policy. It began as follows: "I once tried voting. I voted against Ronald Reagan, and a lot of good that did…."

I don't imagine that all of my students were thrilled about the voter registration assignment, but not a single student ever complained to me about it. Therefore, I was quite surprised when, early in the spring 1999 semester, Charles Okeke called me into his office. He told me that two of my students had complained to Thomas Brown, the provost and associate vice president for human resources, about my voter registration assignment.

"They claimed that your voter registration requirement violates their First Amendment rights," explained Charles.

"First Amendment rights?" I repeated in astonishment. At least they were trying to apply something from class, I thought. But it seemed like a bit of a stretch.

"That's what they told the provost," replied my department chair. "They want him to refund their course fees."

"Isn't it past the deadline to get a refund?"

"Yes," replied Charles. "They are claiming that the deadline should not apply to them, because you have violated their rights."

"But I announced the voter registration assignment on the first day of class. They never said anything to me about objecting to the assignment. Nor did they drop the class. This makes no sense."

"I'm just telling you what Thomas Brown told me. I don't like getting complaints from the provost about faculty in my department."

The comment stung me. "But Charles," I pleaded, "I see my job as inspiring students to get politically involved. Registering to vote is about as minimal a level of involvement as you can get. And I don't even *require* them to register, *per se*. I tell my students that, if they choose not to register, they just need to write me a paragraph explaining why they chose not to."

"These students," replied Charles, "claim that it is none of your business whether or not they register to vote, or what motivation they have. I'm inclined to agree. I want you to rescind the requirement."

I did not have tenure, and in my position, it was not a good idea to disregard an order from my department chair. But he was asking me to compromise my principles, to disregard the main reason why I had chosen to go into this line of work. What was I to do?

I took a deep breath. "Thanks for letting me know about this," I said, deliberately avoiding any commitment to do what Charles had asked.

Fortunately for me, Charles did not demand one. I think he must have assumed that I would do as he had asked. In any case, Charles was chronically overworked, and he was not one to spend any additional time on an issue, once he felt that it had been settled.

I left his office, relieved that I was off the hook for the moment. But I knew that Charles would not forget about this matter. Pretty quickly I would have to find some way out of my moral dilemma.

As luck would have it, I ran into Mike Green. I filled him in on the details. "I just don't understand how Charles could feel that I'm violating my students rights by requiring them either to fill out a voter registration form or to write me a paragraph on why they choose not to. I'm teaching political science, after all. Is this fundamentally different from assigning them an essay on why they support or oppose the right to abortion?"

Mike had listened intently, without once interrupting. Now he cleared his throat. "No it's not fundamentally different. This is a clear-cut issue of academic freedom."

My eyes brightened. "Academic freedom?"

Mike nodded. "It includes being able to choose your teaching methodologies."

"I think you're right. But Charles seems pretty adamant that I eliminate the assignment."

"I think you'll get the support of the faculty if you present this as an issue of academic freedom, and then Charles will have to go along with it. After the controversy over Ringler's course, we'd be hypocrites if we didn't support you on this."

"Jack Ringler? What sort of controversy?"

"A few semesters ago, Ringler proposed teaching a class on the 'New World Order,'" replied Mike.

"International relations after the end of the Cold War? Didn't President Bush coin the phrase in a speech just before the Gulf War?"

Mike nodded.

I was perplexed. "Bush foresaw a world in which the U.S. and Russia would work together, building a new world order based on freedom and democracy. A bit idealistic, perhaps. But why was the course controversial?"

Mike shook his head. "That's not what Ringler's class was about. It focused on a conspiracy by the United Nations to take over the world."

Now I was really confused. "The U.N.? You must be joking."

There was not even the hint of a smile on Mike's face. "That was the theme of his course. Our freedom is under threat, world government is on the way, etc., etc."

"But the U.N. is just about the most inept organization around. I can't see how they'd be capable of taking over the world, when they can't even seem to manage humanitarian aid or peacekeeping very well. Also, aside from the General Assembly — where dozens of powerless statelets get together to pass meaningless resolutions — the U.S. just about runs the U.N. We provide most of its budget. We have a veto in the Security Council. We dominate all the important institutions in the U.N. Hell, the U.N. headquarters is even in New York!"

Mike nodded. "I don't think that we should be teaching students to subscribe to paranoid conspiracy theories. But Ringler's course proposal presented a major philosophical dilemma, and the department argued back and forth about this one. We were stuck between a rock and a hard place." Mike threw up his hands. "I'm all for academic freedom. But I'm still not sure whether we made the right choice."

"Well, at least you have principles."

"Some of us. Others, I suppose, just want to look like they do."

I chuckled.

"This works in your favor," continued Mike. "If I were you, I'd run this by Balboni. If you frame the issue in terms of academic freedom, I think he'll back you up."

"Thanks," I said. "I'm glad I ran into you."

"Don't mention it. But before you go, I have a question for you. It doesn't really matter, when it comes to the main issues at stake. I'm just curious."

I nodded.

"When was the last time these two students came to class?"

I checked my attendance records. "They were there on the first day. I never saw them again after that."

I noticed just a hint of a smile on Mike's face. "Let's review the facts," he said. "Two students come to class on the first day. You never see them again. Weeks go by, and they neither come to class nor drop the class. Finally, they apply for a refund. But it's too late. They've missed the deadline. And they scratch their heads and think to themselves, 'How can we get our money back now?' How, I wonder?"

"Perhaps they can claim that their professor was violating their First Amendment rights?" I laughed. "You're good!"

"I was a reporter, remember?"

I spoke to Al Balboni, as Mike had suggested. Mike had read the situation correctly. Al told Charles that he, personally, would not impose such a requirement on his own students. But then Al went on to insist that I, as an instructor, had the *right* to give my students this assignment. Al insisted that this was an issue of academic freedom, and Charles backed down.

Aside from this single incident, I seemed to have a very good relationship with my department chair. In his evaluation of my

61

performance in February 1999, Charles wrote: "Dr. Lee Miller is an effective faculty [member], a cooperative colleague, [and] a plus [to] the department and the college." He rated my overall performance as "commendable." Charles' evaluation gave me the impression that I would have a smooth journey to tenure. How wrong that impression turned out to be!

In addition to requiring my students to register to vote, I required them to engage in some sort of "political participation activity." They could choose between writing a series of letters to government officials urging some change in public policy, or volunteer work in a government office or with a political organization. Quite a few students chose to do volunteer work. 1998 was an election year, so it was easy for students to find opportunities to volunteer with political parties and election campaigns. In spring 1999, there was no election pending, so I contacted most elected officials and government offices on the local, county, state, and federal level, asking them if they had any interest in volunteers. Not surprisingly, most were very interested in getting college students to work for them on an unpaid basis.

Republican State Senator Mark James was particularly eager to get my students to work in his local office. He dispatched Nathan Taylor, his local district office manager, to each of my classes to recruit students. Senator James was the only member of the state legislature who maintained a local district office. The state provided no funding for such operations, but somehow the senator had secured private donations to maintain a local office. Nathan was a bright and articulate young man, and he also happened to be a student at CCSN. I let Nathan address each of my classes for five minutes, and quite a few students decided to fulfill their political participation requirements by volunteering in Senator James's office.

Several elected officials whom I contacted about accepting volunteers asked me if it would be possible for the students to work as interns. Interns normally have a more significant time commitment than volunteers, and they receive course credit for their work.

I consulted with Charles Okeke. My department chair was supportive, and told me that we could put a Political Science 295 course in the summer schedule. Interns would be able to sign up for this course to get credit for their internships.

In February, I applied for a School to Careers Mini-grant, funded by the federal government, to support the creation of a political internship program at CCSN. No such program had ever existed before, and Charles signed the application, endorsing my plan. More than twenty elected officials and government offices asked to participate in the program. My grant application was approved on March 2.

Tanya Washington, an African American minister's wife and mother of nine, did not wait for my grant to be approved. In early February, she had applied for an internship with U.S. Senator Harry Reid's office. Reid's office accepted her, and she began her internship right away. I consulted with Charles, and he told me that Tanya could sign up for the internship class in the summertime, and receive retroactive credit for her internship work. I was pleased that my department chair was both flexible and fair.

Right after my grant was approved, I sent out an e-mail to all faculty members at CCSN announcing the internship course and asking them to pass on the information to their students. I also prepared written instructions to be distributed to participating students and to the offices in which they would intern. In addition, I prepared a course syllabus, to which Charles gave his verbal approval.

Within the next few days, half-a-dozen students had requested information on the internship course. I mailed them each a copy of the instructions and course syllabus that I had prepared. The deadline for course registration was not until June, and I anticipated plenty of additional students signing up for the course over the next three months.

I expected this internship program to give me a higher profile at the college, easing my way to tenure. But what really excited me was that this program would encourage increasing numbers of students to get involved in politics and public policy. I enjoyed teaching, but what really thrilled me about my job was the opportunity to replace apathy with interest in the political system. I measured my success as a teacher not by the quality of my students' work, but by the passion that they developed.

I really felt that I was inspiring my students to get involved in politics when I was able to convince half a dozen of them to run for Student Government. Norman Schilling filled out the paperwork, but was ineligible because he wasn't enrolled in enough classes. But several other students mounted serious campaigns. Among them were Tanya Washington, the Reid intern, and Mark Leichty, a bright young man who worked part-time in audiovisual services. Mark had videotaped the Regents meeting during which Steve Sisolak had questioned UNR President Joe Crowley.

VI

A Great Educational Opportunity

During the 1998–99 academic year, my most significant and most controversial project was the European political tour. In October 1998, I met with Charles to discuss with him an idea about a summer course on European politics. I proposed to take a group of students to Europe to meet with officials of the European Union. Charles told me that he thought it was a great idea, and suggested that I make the trip a component of a four-credit course. This way, I could then teach one four-credit section of American government in addition to the European course over the summer. CCSN faculty were permitted to teach no more than eight credits over the summer.

Charles asked me to produce a syllabus. I designed the course so that the students would have extensive readings and an exam before departure to Europe, and would write a research paper upon their return. Charles was impressed with my plans, and gave me the go-ahead to make the arrangements.

I was thrilled that Charles had given his blessing. The highlight of my undergraduate studies had been spending my junior year at Oxford University in England. This experience had opened my eyes to the world beyond the United States and sparked my passion for European politics. Oxford was made up of several dozen colleges surrounded by medieval walls. I loved the quaint ceremonies and the bicycle rides and hikes through the lovely countryside surrounding the university. But the most exciting part was the extraordinary access that Oxford students had to policymakers. Members of the Oxford Union (debating) Society had the opportunity to debate members of Parliament and other dignitaries every week. Members of the Oxford University Strategic Studies Group (OUSSG) met with ambassadors from different countries each week to discuss international relations. I loved being a member of each of these institutions.

The highlight of my membership of OUSSG was a trip to Brussels, Belgium. On this trip, we visited both NATO and the Supreme Headquarters Allied Powers Europe, where we held discussions with some of the ambassadors and top military officers leading the alliance. At one point, I recall an ambassador explaining in great detail the plans in place to respond to a Soviet invasion of Europe. "If the Soviets attack West Germany," he explained, "British and American troops will reinforce the Germans to repel the attack. If the Soviets instead attack Turkey, Greek forces will serve as reinforcements."

At that point I raised my hand to ask a question. "Which side will they reinforce?" I asked. Everyone in the room burst into laugher, aside from the ambassador, whose face turned red from embarrassment. All the members of OUSSG were well aware of the hatred that the Greeks and the Turks had for one another.

After returning to the United States the following year to complete my degree at Brandeis University, I wrote an honors thesis on European integration. This work received an award from the Department of Politics. A few years later, I met at a conference one of the professors who had supervised my honor thesis research. He had by that point written several books on the European Union. I was flattered beyond belief when he told me that it was my work that had sparked his interest in the subject.

Taking CCSN students on my proposed trip would be a dream come true. I would have the opportunity to share with my students the events and institutions that had inspired me to go to graduate school. I could not wait. It was my sincere hope that some of them would come to share my fascination and excitement with European political and economic integration.

I wrote to Senator Reid, outlining what I had proposed, and asked for his assistance in making the diplomatic arrangements. With the help of Senator Reid's staff, I was able to arrange meetings with officials at the main institutions of the European Union: the Commission, the Council, and the Parliament in Brussels; the European Court of Justice in Luxembourg; and the European Central Bank in Frankfurt. In addition, we were able to arrange meetings at NATO and at the War Crimes Tribunal for the Former Yugoslavia, as well as with officials of the Dutch and French governments.

By the start of the spring semester in late January 1999, the itinerary was beginning to solidify. It was at this time that I first met Bill Cassell.

Cassell was the most controversial administrator at CCSN, aside, perhaps, from CCSN President Richard Moore. Cassell was a friend and colleague of Moore's from Santa Monica College in California, where Moore had served as president for the twenty years prior to Moore's presidency of CCSN. In 1996, according to newspaper reports, Moore lured Cassell away from Santa Monica College by creating for him the position of associate vice president for international student programs, and by offering him an $85,000 annual salary.[1]

In August 1997, *Las Vegas Review-Journal* reporter Natalie Patton wrote a series of articles focused on the efforts of Cassell and his wife Ilse to recruit foreign students to CCSN.[2] A storm of controversy arose when Patton reported that CCSN had spent $320,000 of taxpayers' money during the 1996–97 academic year on foreign student recruitment efforts. The Cassells had traveled to quite a number of European and Asian destinations, including Finland, France, Sweden, Indonesia, Hong Kong, and Thailand, staying in $200 per night hotels, and collecting $200 per day to use toward meals and other expenses. In addition, Mrs. Cassell was paid $100 per day as a "consultant." Patton quoted Bill Cassell in an August 8, 1997 article as saying the following: "I don't do this because I like to travel. If anyone thinks visiting Taipei and Seoul is a vacation, I have news for them."

Patton's articles also hinted at shady financial dealings associated with the program. She reported that Bill Cassell had contracted with a private company — rather than using CCSN faculty — to provide intensive English instruction for the foreign students. CCSN received $70 per student from the company, funds that went into a special account to be used at the discretion of administrators, rather than being used to pay for the cost of campus facilities used by the company.

CCSN officials claimed that they made a profit on the international student recruitment efforts, because non-residents of Nevada — whether foreign or domestic — paid $4,500 in nonresident tuition. In fact, according to Patton's articles, this money did not go directly to CCSN, but instead into the coffers of the state college system. Furthermore, it cost CCSN approximately $4,500 per student, on average, to provide educational and support services. In other words, it appeared that CCSN was losing money, rather than making money, on the international student recruitment efforts.

Despite all this, Cassell and Moore ultimately weathered the storm of controversy with the program intact.

I met Bill Cassell in January 1999, at a forum exploring the possibility of establishing a study abroad program at CCSN. Sociology Professor Linda Foreman, president of the CCSN chapter of the Nevada Faculty Alliance (NFA), had organized the forum. Linda had personally invited me to attend the forum because she knew that I was in the midst of organizing the European political trip.

Bill Cassell was the keynote speaker at the forum. He trumpeted the success of the study abroad programs he had established at Santa Monica College. He told the assembled professors that he hoped to establish a similar program at CCSN. It struck me as peculiar that someone so successful spoke with so little enthusiasm. I don't think that he smiled even once.

Despite Cassell's dour demeanor, I was enthusiastic about the subject of his talk. When he had finished, Linda said that she was looking for faculty members who would like to work with her to establish a study abroad program at CCSN. I raised my hand: "This summer I'm organizing a program in which CCSN students will spend two weeks in Europe meeting with officials at important European political and legal institutions, like the European Commission, NATO, and the Yugoslav War Crimes Tribunal. I think it would be great if we could establish a study abroad program in Brussels. That's where most of the institutions of the European Union and NATO are located, and also within a few hours drive from the capitals of half a dozen

European countries. It would be the best place in the world to study political science."

Bill Cassell looked down at me with what appeared to be a disdainful expression. "No, that wouldn't work at all," he grumbled. "You don't know what you're doing. You wouldn't be able to attract any students. You have to locate the program in a prime tourist destination, like London or Paris."

"What a prick!" I thought. But I could not afford to alienate an associate vice president, so I just nodded and bit my tongue.

After Cassell left, Linda urged me to get involved. She suggested that maybe we could create a program in Brussels after first establishing a successful program in London or Paris. I shrugged off Cassell's insulting remarks, and agreed to work with her on it.

In the meantime, however, I had a lot of work still to do in preparation for my own study abroad program. I consulted with several colleagues who had taken students to Europe in the past, and they all recommended that I make the travel arrangements with EF Customized Tours. I took their advice. Initially I had planned for the trip to occur in late May, right after the end of the spring semester, but scheduling problems forced me to postpone it until mid-July.

EF specialized in organizing student tours. The tour would include all air and ground transportation, hotel accommodations, tour guides, breakfast and dinner daily, and a multilingual tour director who would accompany us throughout the trip. The price depended on the number of participants. This was because certain costs — like the motorcoach and tour guides—were fixed, regardless of the number of participants. I advertised the cost at $2,999 per participant, based on an expected enrollment of twenty.

I spent an enormous amount of time advertising the trip. I put up flyers on the three main CCSN campuses, plus the two satellite campuses. I wrote to the principals of all high schools in the county, asking them to pass on the information to graduating seniors. I even wrote to personally invite each of the members of the state legislature to go on this trip.

EF's standard contract included one unusual provision: the group leader would receive one free ticket for every six paying participants. Given the amount of work I was putting into organizing this trip (averaging some twenty hours per week, November – April), I figured that I deserved a free ticket for myself. But I felt kind of funny about getting additional free tickets—especially if the enrollment were to fall below the twenty participants at which I had priced the trip, thereby forcing all participants to pay a higher price. I pondered this problem, and came up with what I thought, at the time, was a great solution. I sent an e-mail to all faculty, offering them one free ticket if they could convince six of their students to sign up for the trip. This offer, I figured, would help to boost the enrollment beyond twenty, while at the same time freeing me from the moral dilemma of profiting from the trip.

The response from CCSN faculty was very positive. I received a large number of e-mails from faculty members seeking more information. Al Balboni even sent me a tongue-in-cheek message suggesting that I had great potential for a career in marketing.

Quite a few students also called me to ask for more information about the trip. A woman whom I'll call Gertrude was one of the most memorable.

"Dr. Miller?" asked the voice at the other end of the phone.

"Yes," I replied.

"My name is Gertrude. I'm a student at the West Charleston campus. It is an honor to talk to you. I just saw your flyer, and I can't believe that you're making a trip like this available to students at CCSN."

I smiled, flattered. "Well, it took quite a bit of work, but I had some help from Senator Reid's office."

"It's just incredible, what you've planned. I'm a grandmother from Detroit. I've been all over the world. But this trip you've organized sounds fabulous. I'd expect professors at the University of Michigan to be organizing something like this. You're just wonderful to offer an opportunity like this to students here at CCSN."

I chuckled. "Well, I don't see any reason why students here deserve any less than students at the University of Michigan. If I *can* offer this to CCSN students, then in my opinion, I *should*."

"You know," she continued, "I'm retired now. But I have a lot of experience in public relations, and I talk to everyone. I'd really like to help you out. It would be a dream for me to go on your trip, but I don't think that I can afford it right now. But I think the world of you, and I want to help you promote this trip. I'm going to tell all the students that I can about it. I work in the Counseling Department and at the International Student Center. I bet a lot of the students I talk to would be interested in going. And I'll tell you what. I'd really like it if you would come down to the Charleston campus. I'll introduce you to a bunch of professors who are my friends. I bet we can convince them to announce your trip in their classes."

Gertrude was indeed very convincing. I agreed to meet her that Friday, January 29, at the International Student Center. Gertrude was easy to spot. She was talking nonstop — a slender, white-haired African-American woman. "Are you Gertrude?" I asked shyly.

"Dr. Miller!" she cried, embracing me. "I knew it was you!"

She turned to the student working beside her. "This is Dr. Miller," she announced excitedly. "He's the professor who organized the great trip that I was telling you about."

Gertrude proceeded to introduce me to all of the students in the International Student Center, and then took me to speak to a couple of students who were sitting outside, enjoying the sun. Then Gertrude pulled me aside and chatted alone with me for a while.

"I love being a student here at CCSN! It's changed my life. My life used to be a soap opera. I arrived in Las Vegas a couple of years ago, broke, and emotionally wrecked. Somehow I found my way to the welfare office and was rescued from becoming a bag lady. That was back in February 1997. I was thankful, but I got really depressed living in a retirement home, surrounded by old people who spent day after day complaining constantly about their aches and pains. I felt like everyone was dying, and they were pulling me down with them. It was a miracle was when I found CCSN in May 1997! The moment I became a student, I felt like I was reborn. Vice President Arlie Stops became one of my mentors. He was so kind, always encouraging me. He saw to it that I got into the work study program. The wages have been a lifeline to me. But even more important has been the opportunity to interact in my job with the enthusiastic young people at this college. They've kept me young, and now I finally have enough credits to graduate. Imagine an old lady like me walking with those young kids to receive my diploma at graduation! It's a miracle!"

I was charmed by her enthusiasm. "You're a remarkable woman, Gertrude."

She grabbed my hand and led me back inside. "I want to introduce you to my boss, Bill Cassell, the head of the International Student Center," she said. Before I had time to protest, this little old lady had dragged me into Cassell's office. She proceeded to introduce me to him.

Cassell ground his teeth. "I read your e-mail about the free trips. You're going about this all wrong," he announced brusquely.

My jaw dropped. "What?"

"You can't do things like this. You're setting a bad precedent."

I felt a powerful impulse to hit this arrogant man, but instead I took a deep breath, and smiled. "I'm sorry you feel that way. I think that I'm giving students a great opportunity."

"You can't go through with this," he growled.

This was nearly more than I could bear. "Thanks for sharing your opinion," I said, a bit coldly. Then I walked out the door.

Gertrude seemed unfazed. She grabbed my arm. "Come on, I want to introduce you to some professors I know."

I was annoyed by Cassell's attack, but Gertrude was not a woman to whom you could say no. She took me to the offices of half a dozen professors, who listened to her talk about my trip. Neither the professors nor I were able to get in more than a word or two. It took several hours before Gertrude paused long enough for me to thank her and excuse myself. She promised to keep promoting the trip.

Meanwhile, I worked on contacting the media. I had some success. An article about the upcoming trip appeared in the *Las Vegas Sun* on February 10, 1999, and another article appeared in *Las Vegas City Life* the following day. In addition, several members of the state legislature contacted me to inquire about going on the trip.

The response from my students, however, was more ambivalent. Many of them were extremely excited about the prospect of going on this trip—or at least until they learned the cost. The $2,999 price tag was beyond the reach of most of my students.

I was very upset about this. I had grown up poor, experiencing time on welfare, food stamps, and school lunches subsidized by the taxpayers. I had paid for college without a dime's worth of support from my parents. I had worked many jobs, had taken out enormous student loans, and had earned a number of scholarships. I could not have gone to college, had it not been for the scholarships. Oxford would have been beyond my reach as well. These educational experiences had turned my life around, had opened my eyes to the world, had given me opportunities that I had never dreamed of. It broke my heart to think that underprivileged kids in Las Vegas would be denied this opportunity due to the lack of funds.

In late January 1999, Cheryl Fortezzo-Miller, a CCSN staff member, suggested a solution to me. She said that the Student Government had an annual budget of more than half a million dollars, and that their primary responsibility was to give away this money in ways that benefit students at CCSN. In past years, they had given money for students to go on trips, including some trips to Europe. Why don't I ask them to provide scholarships for needy students, she suggested. In fact, she even introduced me to a student senator named Maurice Norrise.

Maurice, a young African American man with a part-time job in the college print shop, was very enthusiastic about the project. "This would be a great educational opportunity for students," he told me, "a much better thing to spend our money on than another party." At Maurice's urging, I filled out the paperwork to request that the Student Government fund scholarships for six needy students.

The Student Government met every other Friday. My proposal was not included in the agenda on the next meeting date. I inquired why it had been omitted. The secretary in the Student Government office referred me to a stocky, mustached man in his twenties. Dave Abramson, treasurer of the Student Government, informed me that, in order to be included in the agenda, the proposal needed to receive sponsorship signatures from at least three senators. So far, only Maurice had signed.

"This sounds like a good project," said Dave. "But I have some concerns about it. Several senators are uncomfortable about that offer you made to the faculty, that you would give them a free ticket if they get six of their students to sign up."

"Oh," I said, scratching my head. "The tour company's standard contract gives the faculty member organizing the trip one free trip for every six paid participants. I didn't think it was fair for me to hang onto those tickets for myself, so I offered them to other professors. But I don't see why I can't offer the same thing to the Student Government. What if —"

"No, we couldn't accept free trips," interrupted Dave.

"No, no, that's not what I mean. What I was going to suggest is that, for every six students whom you give a scholarship, I'll provide a free trip to an additional needy student."

Dave nodded his head. "That sounds like a step in the right direction. Okay, I'll sign off on your proposal."

Dave added his signature to the form. Several days later, a third senator signed off, and my funding request got onto the agenda for the February 26 Student Government meeting.

I told my classes about the funding request, and urged interested students to attend the meeting. A couple of my students showed up, including Mark Leichty, the student who had videotaped the Regents meeting at which Steve Sisolak had criticized UNR President Joe Crowley.

The meeting was scheduled for 3:00 p.m. The Student Government conference room was empty, aside from my two students and me. No members of the Student Government were present. We waited for several minutes, but no one else showed up. I checked with the secretary in the Student Government office. She assured me that a meeting was scheduled for 3:00, and said that sometimes members of the Student Government were not on time.

At 3:10, Maurice Norrise arrived. He was the senator who had originally urged me to apply for the funds. He said that he wasn't sure why everyone was so late. We chatted some more about the proposal, and then after ten minutes, he set off in search of his colleagues. He returned a few minutes later, alone, unable to explain where the other Student Government members were. Several additional minutes later, a few more members and Larry Braxton, the Student Government advisor, arrived.

Braxton was a tall African American man, about fifty years old, with a deep voice and a head shaved completely bald. He sat down at the end of the room, and a young African American woman whispered to him for a few minutes. Then she cleared her throat.

The young woman was Sandra Ransey, who went by the nickname Niecey, president of the CCSN Student Government. She called roll.

"We have no quorum, so no action we take today can be binding," she announced in a tone of voice laced with boredom. "We will now start the meeting."

First they discussed the minutes from the previous meeting, and other procedural matters. Then they moved on to new business.

"Dr. Miller," she said sternly, "you may now address the senate on your proposal. Your remarks will be limited to one minute."

At that point my students raised their voices in protest. "We've been waiting here for more than half an hour," said Mark. "There's no one else here to speak besides us. I don't see why you can only give Dr. Miller one minute to speak."

"Fine," said Niecey in annoyance. "Dr. Miller may have two minutes."

As quickly as I could, I summarized the details of the planned European trip. "Several bright students have told me that they can't afford to go on the trip, and when I mentioned this to Senator Maurice Norrise, he had urged me to apply for funding from the Student Government for these needy students. I've asked for funding for six students. If you approve this request, I'm prepared to provide a free trip for a seventh student. I thank you for taking the —"

Niecey had been glancing every few seconds at her watch during my two-minute presentation, and finally she interrupted.

"Your time is up," she said. "Do any senators have any comments?"

One young man raised his hand. "The chair recognizes Senator Verley," said Niecey.

"I'd just like to say, for the record, that I oppose this proposal. I mean, we're an American community college. I don't see why we should be spending money to send students to learn about foreign countries. They should be learning about America. If the proposal was to send them to Washington to learn about our government, then I might support it. But not to learn about Luxembourg or some place like that."

"Thank you, Senator Verley," said Niecey warmly, not once glancing at her watch. Are there any other comments? Seeing none, we will move on to the next item on our agenda."

I stood up. "I apologize for interrupting, Madam President," I said respectfully, "but I have a question."

She sighed impatiently. "What's your question?"

"Now that I've made my formal presentation, what do I do next?"

"You lobby us," she said in a voice saturated with sarcasm. Then she moved on to the next matter on the agenda.

I exited quietly from the room, followed by my students.

"I can't believe how rude she was!" exclaimed Mark, as soon as we were out in the hall.

"Me neither," I said.

"I don't know how someone like that can get elected to represent us."

"Apathy on the part of the electorate, probably," I replied. "Maybe you should consider running for office."

The next week, I told each of my classes about my experience at the Student Government meeting. I passed out sheets of paper listing the members of the Student Government, and how to get in touch with them. "Here's a great opportunity for some political action," I told them. "If this is an issue that interests you, call or write to your representatives to let them know what you think." I didn't think that many students would bother, but I felt it was my job to try to get them interested in political action.

It turns out that my announcement coincided with a story in the *Coyote Press*, the CCSN student newspaper, critical of the Student Government. The *Coyote Press* had a history of bad blood with the Student Government. A few years earlier, after a series of unflattering stories, the Student Government had cut off funding for the newspaper. Thereafter, the publication had been forced to rely on the English Department for support. This time, the *Coyote Press* had reported that the Student Government had voted to spend several thousand dollars to extend the water lines into the Student Government office in order to install a sink. This report had followed earlier bad publicity about the senators voting large sums of money to send themselves on various excursions. My students had read about these scandals, and sixty or seventy of them felt obliged to contact their representatives, urging them to support the proposed scholarships as a responsible use of student funds.

By far, the most active was Calvin Chadwick. Cal was a man in his thirties, with a long blond pony-tail and a very relaxed demeanor. He was divorced and re-married, with several young children. He had been a nightclub manager for some big chain, and had been transferred to Las Vegas a couple of years earlier. Apparently, the Las Vegas club had gone out of business, and Cal had been left without a job. He had decided to go back to school to earn his college degree. Cal was a good student, and a very hard worker. He was also extremely eager to go on the European trip, and he made the scholarship issue his personal crusade.

Cal made it a point to go down to the Student Government office and lobby the senators in person on several occasions. He even asked me for the phone numbers of the other scholarship applicants, and coordinated joint lobbying efforts with them. He always showed up at the Student Government meetings at which the issue was scheduled to be discussed.

The following Friday, March 5, my department held its election for chair. Charles Okeke ran unopposed, and was duly elected. I felt very good about voting for him. Thus far, he had been very supportive of most of my endeavors. It was a vote that I later came to regret.

The next Student Government meeting was scheduled for March 12. I showed up, along with several of my students. Again there was no quorum, and as a result, no vote was taken on my funding request.

On the following Monday, March 15, I went to speak to Dave Abramson, the Student Government treasurer. He told me that he had some concerns about my proposal, and we went to consult with Joe Carter, the CCSN administrator who served as financial advisor to the Student Government.

"Mr. Carter," said Dave, "Dr. Miller has proposed that we spend about $18,000 to send six students on his political science trip to Europe. What do you think about this? Is this likely to get us into trouble?"

"It's not my place to advise you on the merits of the proposal," said Carter. "That's for the Student Government to decide. But I don't think there's anything in your constitution that would forbid you from allocating the funds for this, if you want to."

"But the Regents have been breathing down our necks since we paid for some senators to go on some of the trips we funded. I don't want this to happen again."

"Then you should make sure that members of the Student Government don't go on this trip," suggested Carter.

"I think that we have a problem with a conflict of interest here, Dr. Miller," said Dave, playing with the end of his mustache. "There's a problem if *you* pick the students we fund to go on the trip. We have the same problem if *we* pick them. There's not enough money for us to send everyone on this trip. I don't know how we can avoid this. Could we maybe have other faculty besides you pick the students?"

"You could have a faculty selection committee," suggested Carter.

"Okay," said Dave. "Dr. Miller, this is what I want you to do. I will throw my support behind your proposal, and by doing so, I can pretty much guarantee you that it will pass. What I want you to do is advertise the scholarships. Let everyone know that they should apply for the scholarships if they want to go on the trip."

"I could send another e-mail to all the faculty," I offered.

"Good. You do that, and prepare some sort of application."

"In my funding proposal, I said that only needy students would be eligible. I guess I could ask them to verify that they are receiving need-based financial aid, or give some other evidence of financial need. Maybe I could also require them to write an essay about why they want to go on the trip, and get a letter of recommendation from a faculty member."

"Yeah, that sounds good. Mr. Carter?"

Carter nodded.

"Okay, so you advertise the scholarships," said Dave, "and I'll make sure they pass. When we get the applications, we'll know how many people are interested, and we'll have a better idea of how much money to allocate. Right now, let's say we allocate $20,000, say $1,000 per student for twenty students."

I nodded my head, pleased at his support.

"I want you, Dr. Miller, to set up a selection committee of faculty members," continued Dave. "You should *not* be a member. That way we'll avoid a conflict of interest. The committee should meet and rank-order the applicants before our next Student Government meeting, on March 26. Then we can fund the scholarships, but we won't be the ones selecting the recipients." Dave looked at Carter. "And I'll make sure to put a clause in the motion that Student Government members aren't eligible to receive funds to go on this trip. How does that sound?"

"That should be fine," said Carter.

"Thanks," I said.

"One more thing," said Dave. "It would really smooth things out if your colleague, Dr. Balboni, would endorse this proposal. He commands a lot of respect. Do you think you could ask him for me?"

"Sure, I'll ask him," I said. We all shook hands, and I departed.

As soon as I got back to my office, I sent the following e-mail to the "everyone" list, which included all CCSN employees:

Faculty, please inform your students:

There will likely be several scholarships available for needy students wishing to go on the political science trip to Europe. Recipients will be selected based on financial need and academic performance/promise. Application instructions may be picked up at the Department of Philosophical and Regional Studies, Cheyenne Campus, room 2022. If you have any questions, please feel free to call me. Application deadline is 5 p.m. on Thursday, March 25.

Lee Miller

Ext. 4089

I printed a stack of application instructions, which conformed to the requirements I had discussed with Dave Abramson and Joe Carter. The instructions listed the price of the trip, and left it open for the applicants to specify how much financial assistance they would need to be able to afford the trip. I left the stack of papers on Venus' desk, with a note asking her to give a copy to anyone who requested one.

The next day, I announced the scholarships to my students, and many asked for application instructions. I got a bunch of phone calls and e-mails from other interested persons. Even Al Balboni, the busy chair of the Faculty Senate, got involved. He cc'd me with an e-mail he had sent to a couple of his best students, urging them to apply for the scholarships.

I called up Al and thanked him. "Oh, by the way," I said. "It was Dave Abramson who asked me to go ahead and advertise the scholarships. When I spoke with him, he said that it would help him get it passed if you were to come out in favor of it."

Al sighed. "Lee, I support your efforts, but as chair of the Faculty Senate, I can't take a stand on things like this. It wouldn't be proper."

"I understand entirely," I replied. "But I told Dave that I would ask you. I'll let him know what you said."

Given that Al wished to take a hands-off approach to this issue, I figured that he probably would prefer not to serve on the committee. So I spoke to three other professors in my department — Billy Monkman, Mark Rauls, and Fran Campbell — and all three agreed to serve on the committee.

Everything was coming together, I realized excitedly. Dozens of students would have the educational opportunity of a lifetime. I could not have been happier. Nor could I have been more naïve.

VII

No Good Deed Goes Unpunished

I called up Dave Abramson, and let him know that all the arrangements were in place. He sounded strangely upset when I told him that Al Balboni felt that he could not take a position with regard to my funding request. But I did not have the time to give it much thought. I had to get ready for class, and I still had one more call to make.

I called Gertrude and told her about the Student Government meeting. She eagerly offered to call Niecey Ransey, the Student Government president, to urge her to support the scholarship proposal.

The following day, Gertrude called me back. She told me that Niecey had been rude to her on the phone, and that the girl had badmouthed me. Gertrude said that she had demanded to speak to the Student Government advisor. When Braxton got on the phone, he was equally rude. Gertrude told me, "I chewed them out with my big mouth. 'How dare you speak badly of Dr. Miller! He's doing a great thing for students at this college, and you should kiss the ground he walks on for the privilege of working at the same institution as a great man like Dr. Miller!'"

I did not know what to think. It was nice of Gertrude to stand up for me, but I could not figure out why Niecey or Braxton would hold any animosity toward me. I thanked Gertrude for letting me know what had transpired, and hung up the phone. I was perplexed and unsettled.

Soon thereafter, I ran into Maurice Norrise, the student senator who had originally urged me to apply for the funding. "I still think that these scholarships are a great idea," he told me. "But it would probably be better if I distance myself from this project. Mr. Braxton, our advisor — he hates me, and so does Niecey. They'd like nothing better than to find a way to kick me off the senate. If your proposal gets too closely associated with me, it may run into trouble."

"But Mr. Braxton is your advisor. Why would he try to thwart a project just because you support it?"

"I don't know. But I do know that he badmouths me behind my back to the other senators. Several of them have told me about this."

"Has anyone said anything to you about my proposal?"

"Yeah," said Maurice. "Braxton and Niecey gave me a lot of grief about encouraging you to apply for funding. They said that I'm supposed to be neutral, and not support anything until after we've discussed it first in the senate."

"That's ridiculous!" I exclaimed. "You have to sign the proposal for it to get on the agenda. How do they expect you to sign something if you don't support it? There would be no way for anything to get on the agenda."

"I know," said Maurice. "This is crazy. But if you want your proposal to pass, I'd better lay low for a while."

I sighed, utterly perplexed by these revelations. "Thanks," I said, "I'll keep this in mind."

It wasn't long before I ran into Braxton himself. "Lee," he said in a voice tinged with hostility, "your proposal is in trouble. If I were you, I'd just drop the whole thing right now. Your request has gotten associated with Maurice, and everyone on the Student Government hates him. If Maurice supports something, it's the kiss of death. This thing is never going to pass, and if I were you, I'd just forget about it."

"But Dave Abramson told me he supports it," I offered. "It's a good proposal. It'll benefit the students."

"Look," growled Braxton, "I'm telling you this for you own good. You should drop this thing right now. I'm telling you that it is going nowhere. Got it?"

"Uh-huh," I mumbled, and walked away. I was too shocked to be angry. I could not believe that the Student Government advisor, of all people, would speak badly to me of one of the students he was advising. And why was he so hostile to my funding request?

On Tuesday, March 23, I received another cc of an e-mail from Al Balboni to a couple of his students. It read something like this: "I'm sorry that I misinformed you. There will be no scholarships for the European trip. Do not apply. Sorry for any inconvenience this may have caused you." My heart dropped into my stomach.

I called up Al right away. "I got your e-mail," I said, struggling to take a breath. "What's this about there not being any scholarships?"

"I just came from a meeting between Dr. Silverman and the Faculty Senate leadership," said Al, a bit coldly. "He told us that there will be no scholarships for the trip to Europe."

"What?" I gasped, baffled. "This is the first I've heard of this. What's going on?"

"I can't say. I suggest you give Silverman a call. Oh, and Lee, I'm pretty angry that you told Dave Abramson that I endorsed your scholarship proposal. I told you very clearly that I couldn't take a stand on this."

I gasped again. "But I told Dave what you said, that you felt that, as Faculty Senate chair, it was improper for you to take a stand on it."

"That's not what he told Silverman. Silverman said that Dave had told him that I had endorsed this thing."

"This is crazy," I said. I felt like someone had transported me to an alternative universe where all the laws of physics worked backwards. I was thoroughly confused.

I called Silverman right away. His secretary put me on hold for a moment, and then connected me.

Silverman did not even say hello. "This scholarship thing is getting out of hand!" the senior vice president shouted at me over the phone. "You're not following appropriate procedures! You're setting all sorts of bad precedents! You have conflicts of interest! What do you think you're doing?"

I was shocked speechless. But Silverman did not pause for me to answer his charges.

"The Student Government should have nothing to do with this thing!" Silverman continued yelling at me. "If a student can't afford your trip, then he should go to the Financial Aid office! Not the Student Government! Are you crazy? I want you to go down to Financial Aid right away and speak to Chemene Crawford. She'll set you straight on all this. Then I want you to get your butt in here and meet with me about this thing. You'd better start working through the appropriate channels, or you're going to be in a *lot* of trouble!"

I was trembling from the outburst. "Okay," I whimpered.

Silverman hung up.

I tended to come unglued when someone started yelling at me. I just was no good at angry confrontations. Rather than yelling back, or articulating a thoughtful and measured response, I just would start to tremble and stumble over my words. My father had a violent temper when I was a kid, and he scared the hell out of me when he started to yell. When angry words began to fly, hard objects were likely to fly after them. Fortunately for me, he seemed to have very bad aim. But that did little to dampen my terror. So, when Silverman screamed at me, my heart started to race and my hands to shake. Some things you just do not grow out of.

I hung up the phone and took some deep breaths, waiting for my heart rate to slow. When I'd pulled myself together, I called Linda Foreman, president of the Nevada Faculty Association (NFA, the professional association representing the interests of faculty with the college administration and with government officials) and told her what had transpired. "What is this all about?" I asked her, my voice still quaking a bit.

"I'm not sure," she said. "I'll give Bob a call. He's been yelling a lot at faculty members lately. I think that Richard Moore is putting him under a lot of pressure. Bob's going to end up having a heart attack or a stroke if he keeps this up. But that's no excuse. He shouldn't be yelling at you. I'll give him a call."

I thanked Linda. After hanging up, I took some more deep breaths to calm myself.

Next I went down to the Financial Aid office, and asked to speak to Chemene Crawford, the director of Financial Aid, as Silverman had instructed. The student at the counter said that Crawford was unavailable, and she referred me to Bernadette Lopez-Garrett, a financial aid advisor. Lopez-Garrett told me that Crawford would be out of town for the next several days.

"I hope you can help me," I said urgently, leaning forward across the counter. "Dr. Silverman asked me to meet with Ms. Crawford. It's really important. Could I maybe speak to her boss?"

"That would be Arlie Stops," said Lopez-Garrett. "He's associate vice president for admissions and financial aid. I'll see if he's available." Lopez-Garrett stepped away from the counter and disappeared into one of the offices behind it. She returned a few moments later. "You're in luck," she said, flashing me a smile. "Follow me."

Arlie Stops was a middle-aged man with deeply-tanned skin and close-cropped hair. He had a warm smile below his neat mustache. I remembered Gertrude telling me that Stops was a very kind and caring man, and that he had been a mentor to her.

I sat down in Stops' office beside Lopez-Garrett. I took a deep breath and forced myself to calm down. I did not want to come across as a lunatic.

I carefully told the pair about the trip I had planned with the help of Senator Reid. "Then I applied for funding from the Student Government," I explained, "because a number of good students couldn't afford to go on this trip. As far as I know, I followed all the procedures correctly. But Dr. Silverman said that the Student Government isn't the right place for needy students to get help with the cost of the trip — that they should be able to get help from the Financial Aid office."

Stops sighed. "It sounds like you're putting together a great program," he said. "It would be a shame if the cost prevented some students from going. But Bob is wrong about them getting financial aid to go on this trip. The only way that we could provide additional financial aid for a student to go on this trip would be if the student had not previously accepted all the aid that he or she was entitled to this year. At this point in the academic year, it is too late for us to increase the aid eligibility for a given student. No matter how expensive this trip is going to be, we can't give those students extra grants or loans to pay for it."

"But what about the Student Government?" I asked. "Is there some reason why they can't provide scholarships?"

"First of all, I'm going to ask you to stop using that term. The word 'scholarship' implies that the Financial Aid Office is involved in disbursing the money. All scholarship funds come through us. But leaving this issue aside for a moment, I see no reason why the Student Government can't provide travel stipends for students who wish to go on your trip. I think that you did the right thing by asking them. The Financial Aid Office can't do anything to help out at this point in the game. Bob was misinformed about the role of Financial Aid. I'm going to give him a call and let him know that I advised you to go ahead with your efforts to get some travel money from the Student Government. As for you, I'd advise you to make sure you follow all the appropriate procedures with the Student Government, and meet with Larry Braxton to make sure that everything goes smoothly."

I sighed with relief, convinced that the problem with Silverman was all some sort of misunderstanding caused by me using the word "scholarship." I thanked Stops and Lopez-Garrett for taking the time to meet with me, and I went back to my office.

Linda Foreman called me up. "I spoke to Silverman," the NFA president told me. "He was pretty angry on the phone. I couldn't quite figure out why. Something about 'process' and 'chain of command.' Anyway, I told him to calm down. I said, 'Bob, you shouldn't be yelling at faculty.' He tried to protest, but I repeated myself. He said something about Jill Derby chewing him out over this."

"Jill Derby, the chair of the Board of Regents? What's she got to do with this?" I asked. The relief I had experienced from my meeting with Stops evaporated.

"I don't know. But Bob also mentioned 'remediation.'"

"Remediation?" I asked. "What's that?"

"Remediation is the procedure they follow before they fire you."

I gasped.

"I'm sure it won't come to that," added Linda quickly. "I think that Bob is just under too much pressure. Just do what he says, and this will all blow over."

I told Linda that I had met with Arlie Stops because Chemene Crawford, the financial aid director, was out of town.

"Good. Make sure you let Bob know. You need to keep the lines of communication open with him."

I thanked Linda, and hung up. I felt like someone had rolled up, like a Persian rug, the landscape of the world I was familiar with, revealing an utterly alien world beneath. If the chair of the Board of

Regents was involved, I was in big trouble. The most unnerving part of it all was that I had absolutely no idea why.

I got in front of my computer and drafted an e-mail to Silverman. I cc'd Stops, Al, and Charles. I went through several drafts, each time purging the message of the powerful emotions that kept slipping in. The version I sent read as follows:

> Thanks for discussing with me this morning your concerns about providing financial assistance for needy students wishing to go on the political science trip to Europe.
>
> I sought out Chemene Crawford, Director of Financial Aid, as you had suggested. Unfortunately, she is out of town until next week. Therefore, I met instead with Associate Vice President Arlie Stops and Ms. Bernadette Lopez-Garrett.
>
> Mr. Stops stated that it was within the powers of the Student Government to fund an activity such as this, and that he thought that my proposal for travel grants was a good one. He said that he planned to let you know that he supports this proposal.
>
> Ms. Lopez-Garrett and Mr. Stops agreed that some confusion had been caused by my use of the word "scholarship," which implies some association with student financial aid. We agreed that it would be better to term the money "travel stipends," since the money will not be used for tuition, but instead be used for transportation and lodging while on the trip.
>
> You had expressed to me concern that I might have a conflict of interest in seeking financial assistance from the CCSN Student Government for needy students. At the Student Government meeting which I attended last month, and in subsequent discussions with Treasurer Dave Abramson, I had agreed to various measures to avoid any conflict of interest.
>
> Members of the Student Government had expressed concern that I would be receiving one free ticket for each six applicants who go on this trip. I responded that any free tickets received because stipend recipients are going on the trip (i.e. one free ticket received for each six stipend recipients) would be given to the selection committee, to be awarded to needy students.
>
> Mr. Abramson has suggested that the Student Government allocate $20,000 to provide $1,000 travel grants for twenty needy students. If his proposal is adopted, I will be able to provide an additional three free trips, to be awarded by the selection committee to students with extreme financial need.

There was also concern about a conflict of interest if I were to serve on the selection committee. I had agreed not to serve on the selection committee. The following faculty members have agreed to serve on the committee: Guillermo Monkman, Mark Rauls, and Fran Campbell.

I hope that this memo has addressed your concerns adequately. I look forward to discussing the matter further with you.

I mouthed a silent prayer as I hit the send button.

The next day, March 24, I faxed Regent Steve Sisolak a copy of the e-mail, along with a letter outlining what had occurred. I called him a few hours later to follow up.

"Lee, I don't know what to say," said Steve. "This is the strangest thing I've ever heard."

"Al Balboni, who has been a mentor to me, has a saying: 'No good deed goes unpunished.' Everything I did, I did for the students. Now, I think Silverman is getting ready to fire me. Linda Foreman, the NFA president, said that he mentioned 'remediation' to her, and that's a prelude to firing." I got all choked up as I said this.

Steve tried to reassure me. "There's no way Bob is going to fire you over this. From what you've told me, I can't figure out what you've done wrong. This makes no sense."

My spirits rose just a bit. Steve, a member of the powerful Board of Regents, was sympathetic. But there was something else still bothering me. "Silverman mentioned to Linda that Jill Derby has been giving him grief over this. What interest would she have in this?"

"I can't imagine," said Steve. "I was planning to call her later today about something else, and I'll ask her then. If you want, I'll give Bob a call too. But it might be better if I stay out of this thing for now. It might make matters worse if I were to get involved. It might look to Bob like you're trying to go over his head."

"You're probably right," I said. I understood his point, but I was disappointed. I had half-hoped that that Steve would offer to call up Silverman and tell him to leave me alone.

"Thanks, Steve," I said. "Please let me know if you find out anything from Jill Derby."

Later that day, I received an e-mail from Silverman:

I asked you to come to the office tOo [sic] talk. I'll ask again. If you want to do this project pr4esent [sic] it to me and Page and Charles and follow procedures. Also, how are you giving credit for an intern class????? Been to curriculum??? Bob

This reply to my carefully worded e-mail was far from comforting. Silverman was accusing me of not following procedures of some sort. That was the sort of thing that might cost me my job. "Damn!" I thought. "I wish I knew what I had done wrong."

I was also perplexed that Silverman had mentioned my internship class in the message about the European trip. I had received a grant, made all preparations, and Charles had approved everything. In this case, I was sure that I had followed all the appropriate procedures, because I had received the list of procedures in writing. Why was Silverman concerned about the internship class at this point, I wondered. Something wasn't right. I suddenly had a premonition of impending doom.

But I told myself that I was being silly. This must all be some big misunderstanding. I had followed all procedures to the best of my knowledge, and my motivations had been unselfish from the start. Everything I had done was for the benefit of the students. All I needed to do was meet with Silverman, I told myself, and get this all sorted out. Then I remembered the way Silverman had screamed at me on the phone, and all my confidence evaporated.

But I had no option other than to meet with him. So I sent an e-mail to Venus, the PRS department secretary, letting her know that Silverman wanted to meet with Charles, Page, and me. ("Page" was Marion Littlepage, dean of curriculum and scheduling.) I told Venus my schedule for Thursday and Friday, and asked her to coordinate everyone's schedules and set up the meeting. I cc'd Silverman, Charles, and Page.

Venus never wrote back to me. But the following day, Thursday, March 25, Charles did, cc'ing Venus, Silverman and Page. Charles wrote that he had decided to cancel my internship course. He said that before he would consider reinstating it, I would have to consult with all the other faculty members in the department in order to form a consensus in favor of it.

"Oh my God!" I gasped. I could not believe what I was reading. Charles had given me his enthusiastic verbal support, as well as his written approval, for the internship course. Now he was reneging on it.

I read on with consternation: "I gave my approval to the European course, independent of, and prior to the much discussed 'Scholarship' scheme. I do not desire to be part of the scheme. I do not want to take part in any meeting where that scheme is to be discussed."

"Holy shit!" I felt like I was being strangled. Silverman had asked Charles and me to meet with him, and Charles had refused. Charles was my department chair, and he refused even to show up at a meeting that might determine whether or not I would be fired. Apparently, Charles was planning to hang me out to dry.

It took me some minutes to regain the ability to speak, rather than just croak like a frog. At that point, I called up JoAnn Zahm, Silverman's secretary, to schedule an appointment. She said that Silverman's schedule was really busy, and that she'd have to get back to me.

The scholarship applications came in the next day. Only six students had applied. I prepared a packet of informational materials on the travel stipends for the Student Government. It included a letter from me describing the planned program and mentioning that Dave had asked me to advertise the travel stipends. It also included a copy of my e-mail advertising the travel stipends, the application instructions, and copies of the applications I had received, with the names blacked out to preserve the privacy of the students.

The Student Government meeting the following day, Friday, March 26, was cancelled due to lack of attendance. The next meeting was scheduled for April 9, two weeks later.

I went to see Larry Braxton, as Stops had advised. Braxton had an office next to that of Thomas Brown, the provost, and across the hall from the Student Government office.

Braxton did not even say hello. "The Student Government meeting was cancelled today," he announced coldly. "They won't be able to discuss your request until April 9."

"I know," I replied, trying hard to sound friendly, despite his apparent hostility. "I just came by to make sure that I'm doing everything properly, and to see if you have any advice for me."

At that moment, a student rushed into the room. "I've got it all set up!" he cried excitedly.

Braxton and the student crowded around Braxton's computer. They spent half an hour exploring the new web site that the student had designed for Braxton. Neither said a word to me, nor even looked in my direction. "How rude!" I thought to myself. "Braxton should have either asked the student to wait, or asked me to come back later." Despite these feelings, I held my tongue and waited patiently. Finally, the student left.

"Still here?" muttered Braxton. I wasn't sure whether he sounded disappointed or annoyed. Probably it was a bit of both.

"Yes," I said, polite but assertive. "I came here to seek the advice of the Student Government advisor. I want to make sure that I'm doing everything properly with regard to my funding request."

"Look," said Braxton, "you filled out the forms and came before the Student Government to answer their questions. As far as I'm concerned, that's all you're supposed to do. I already told you that you should forget about this thing, that your proposal is a dead duck."

I ignored his hostility. "Can you give me any advice on how to smooth things out?"

"Nope." Braxton folded his arms and turned his back on me.

"Bastard!" I thought. I left his office, fuming. My anger soon morphed into worry, however. I worried all weekend. I worried about whether I would fail in my efforts to secure the funding, thereby letting the students down. I worried that there was some bizarre conspiracy going on to prevent it. I worried that this whole thing was going to cost me my job.

On Monday, March 29, I met again with Arlie Stops. "I called Bob Silverman, as I'd promised," he said. "I told Bob that Financial Aid can't provide any additional funds for students going on your trip, and that we can't touch any Student Government money. Bob seemed to be angry at you for some reason."

"Why do you think he was angry at me?" I asked, hoping that Stops might be able to shed some light on this bizarre series of events.

"No idea," he replied. "But if I were you, I'd follow the advice I gave you last time: be careful to go through all the appropriate channels with the Student Government, and meet with Larry Braxton to smooth things out. Also, make sure you avoid any conflicts of interest."

"Thanks. I've already followed your advice. I met with Mr. Braxton. I set up a selection committee made up of three faculty members. I won't serve on the committee."

"Sounds like you're on the right track," said Stops. "Good luck."

"Thanks," I said.

Later that week I called up Steve Sisolak. I told him what had transpired since our previous conversation. There was shocked silence at the other end of the phone line.

Finally, Steve replied: "Lee, I don't know what to tell you. Bob Silverman can get hot under the collar at times, but he's always seemed to be a reasonable guy. If I were you, I'd just go in there and find out what this is all about."

"That's what I'm planning to do. Did you, by any chance, speak to Jill Derby."

"Oh, yeah, I did. She recognized your name. She told me that she got your letter inviting her to go on the European trip, and that it sounded really great, but that she has other commitments. She also said that she never spoke to Bob about you or about your European trip."

"She never spoke to him?" I repeated. "That's really weird. Somebody is lying. I just wish I could figure out who it is, and why."

"I can't help you with that. But keep me posted on what transpires at your meeting."

"Thanks," I said, and hung up.

On Thursday, April 1, I called Linda Foreman. "Lee, you'd better meet with Bob and get this sorted out," she said. "This is getting ugly. Have you scheduled an appointment yet?"

"I spoke to JoAnn last week, and asked her to schedule a meeting. She said she had to get back to me. I haven't heard back from her."

"Then call her again. You've got to get this sorted out before it spins out of control. If you want, I'll try to come to the meeting with you. I'll tell Bob that I'm there as your colleague, rather than in some formal capacity as NFA president."

"I'd really appreciate that, Linda."

"I like you," she said. "I think you're doing great work here. I don't want to lose you." The dark implication of this compliment unsettled me.

I called JoAnn again, as Linda had suggested. "Dr. Silverman has a very busy schedule this week and next," Silverman's secretary told me. "I might be able to squeeze you in on the morning of Thursday, April 15, but I can't promise anything. I'll have to get back to you as the date approaches."

"Please let me know," I said.

I had mixed feelings about this. I was glad that I would be able to put off for a couple of weeks getting screamed at again by Silverman. On the other hand, I was getting very apprehensive about what this all meant for my career.

VIII

The President Speaks

This scholarship controversy was beginning to take its toll on me. I was emotionally drained, and I was falling behind in my work. I put the matter aside for the next five days and caught up with my grading.

Under normal circumstances, grading my students' papers is the part of my job that I like the least. Every semester my students seem to plumb new depths in the misuse of the English language. I can never quite understand why so many papers average six spelling mistakes per page in an era when all my students use word processing software with built-in spell-check. I find it even more perplexing that three or four students per class always seem to misspell the names of the authors whose work they are making reference to. Grammar and syntax problems abound — and not just for students whose first language is something other than English.

I have gotten pretty good at the art of puzzling out the meaning that a student is trying to convey. The process is sort of like what you go through when you have two years of college French and are trying to discern the meaning of a passage from Molière. For example, consider the following sentence: "Hudson proofs Medison wrong and sez that separation of balances make our guvment to unrecountable to the public." Using a combination of familiarity with the material assigned to the class, familiarity with the type of prose that students often turn in, and a great deal of imagination, I was able to come up

94

with the following translation: "Hudson disagrees with Madison, indicating that the separation of powers and checks and balances render our government too unresponsive and too unaccountable to the public."

I grit my teeth and try very hard not to be turned off by my students' abuse of English. As long as I can glean some meaning from a paper, I usually try to grade it based on the insights that it has showcased. I also refer the worst abusers to the Writing Center for extra help on subsequent assignments.

Of course, my greatest frustration is that the majority of students seem to be incapable of following directions. If the directions clearly ask them to do six things, most do only three or four. This can be quite discouraging at times. But it also tends to result in a normal distribution of grades. Those who do all of what I ask get A's, those who do most of it get B's, and so on. Students almost never argue their grades with me, because I am careful to list on each paper the ways in which the author has neglected to do one or more of the things assigned.

Despite all this, I actually was looking forward to climbing the mountain of papers awaiting me. I relished the prospect of spending five days grading my students' papers, a prospect that seemed infinitely more appealing than even one more minute of conversation with the likes of Niecey Ransey, Bill Cassell, Larry Braxton, or Bob Silverman.

This blissful period came to an end on April 6. It was on that day that the travel stipend selection committee met. Fran Campbell bowed out at the last minute, saying that she was too busy. Two applications had come in late. I gave Billy Monkman and Mark Rauls copies of all eight applications, and left the room. Among the applicants were Gertrude, Tanya Washington (the minister's wife who interned with Senator Reid), and Razije Elez, a young ethnic Albanian woman from Yugoslavia, who had a keen interest in our scheduled visit to the Yugoslav War Crimes Tribunal in the Hague, Netherlands.

Billy and Mark deliberated for several minutes behind closed doors before finally coming out to get me. They had rank-ordered the applicants. Billy and Mark signed a memo to the Student Government urging them to award the travel stipends according to the order they had ranked them.

That day I received an envelope from Nathan Taylor, the district office manager for Nevada State Senator Mark James. Senator James was the chair of the Senate Judiciary Committee, and many of my students had worked as volunteers in his district office, under Nathan's supervision. I had asked Nathan if the senator would write a letter to the members of the CCSN Student Government in support of my request for travel stipends. The senator had done so, and Nathan had sent me a copy of the senator's letter. Among other things, it said that the trip "would be a significant experience for students of political science and those interested in the study of comparative political systems. I commend Dr. Miller for his innovation and initiative."

I still had not heard back from JoAnn by Friday, April 9, and I called her a third time to request a meeting with Silverman. She said that she was working on it, and would get back to me.

Later that morning I ran into Dave Abramson. "I'm concerned about a conflict of interest," he said. "Three of the scholarship applicants have filed to run for Student Government. I think this might be a problem. The Regents have been after us before for allocating money for trips that Student Government members go on. Do you think you could get a legal opinion from the system's attorney on this?"

I said I would try. I called up Steve Sisolak, and he gave me the phone number for the Office of the General Counsel for the University and Community College System of Nevada (UCCSN).

I dialed the number, and Assistant General Counsel Kwasi Nyamekye agreed to take a look at things. I faxed him a copy of the Student Government constitution, plus information on the trip and the travel stipend selection procedures. Kwasi advised me that we could make a "good-faith" argument that running for office should not be held against a scholarship applicant. He said that as long as *current* members of the Student Government were not applying for the stipends, it would probably be okay. Furthermore, he told me that he didn't see anything in the Student Government constitution that would prohibit them from providing travel stipends of the sort described in the documents that I had faxed him.

Over the next few days I compiled a packet of materials to present to the Student Government in support of my funding request. In the packet, I included copies of letters from elected officials supporting the project, newspaper articles describing the upcoming trip, and a detailed schedule of meetings to be held with foreign officials.

The Student Government meeting was scheduled for 3:00 p.m. on Friday, April 9. On the morning of that day, I went over to the Student Government office. They had a full-time office manager, plus several students working part-time. I told the office manager that I had some materials that I wanted to pass out to the members of the Student Government. I asked her if she would be able to make a copy for each of the members.

"Sure," she said, smiling. "No problem."

I gave her the packet, and returned to my office, relieved that I could get back to my grading, rather than spending time standing in front of a photocopier.

At 2:40 I walked over to the Student Government office. I asked the office manager whether she had finished the photocopies. She looked upset, and told me that Mr. Braxton wanted to speak with me.

I walked across the hall to Braxton's office. He leaped to his feet as soon as I entered. "How dare you make *my* secretary do *your* copying!" he roared. Braxton rushed toward me and threw a stack of papers onto the table. They scattered this way and that; large numbers spilled out onto the floor.

I flushed. "When I asked her, she told me that she could make the copies! Had she refused, I would have done them myself."

"You had no right to ask her!" snarled Braxton "You should do your own work!"

My hands started to shake. The old Pavlovian response to confrontations was beginning to kick in. "I asked her to make copies of materials to be passed out to the members of the Student Government," I croaked through my tightening throat. "I figured that this was an appropriate request for the Student Government office manager. She agreed!"

"You had no right to ask her!" screamed Braxton. He stormed out of his office, and left me alone to sort through the mess of papers.

I spent ten minutes sorting the disordered mess without making any discernable progress. Finally, I realized that I would never be finished before the meeting was scheduled to start. I hated wasting paper, but what could I do? I dumped the whole load into the recycling bin and rushed back to my office to make fresh sets of copies. I ran as quickly as I could, and I arrived back at the Student Government meeting room at 3:01 p.m.

The room was packed with people. A quorum of Student Government members had shown up for a change. So had a dozen students ready to voice support for my funding proposal. Most of the students who had applied for the travel stipends were there, including Cal Chadwick. Mark Leichty, who had decided to run for Student Government president, was there as well. So was Nathan Taylor, Senator James' district office manager.

I took a look at the agenda for the meeting. It was packed with funding requests. They included $16,000 to help pay for repairs to the gym and for the salaries of students working there, $20,000 to purchase computer equipment for the libraries, $120,000 to purchase new computers for the computer labs, and $25,000 to hold an "End-of-Semester Bash." I wondered why the Student Government felt it necessary to pay for items like new computers and gym repairs, which normally should come out of the college budget.

My request was the first item on the agenda. Niecey called the meeting to order, and then called roll. There was a quorum, for once. The minutes were approved, and then Niecey gazed into the eyes of Braxton, and said the following:

"I think that I speak on behalf of the entire senate and executive board in thanking Mr. Braxton for all the hard work he has done this year, and all the help and guidance that he's given us. Mr. Braxton has been more than just an advisor to us ...." She went on and on oozing praise and admiration for Braxton. When she finally finished, Braxton reciprocated, with an equally saccharine tribute to Niecey's many virtues. Cal rolled his eyes at me.

When this love-fest had finally come to a close, Niecey noticed a bald man in a suit standing just inside the doorway. It was Pete Aleman, dean of Information Technology and Academic Computing. "I want to suggest a change in the agenda," announced Niecey. "Professor Aleman was kind enough to come here today to talk to us about the proposed appropriation for computers for the computer labs. I will entertain a motion to move this item forward, so that we can allow Professor Aleman to get back to his very important work as soon as possible."

Mark leaned over and whispered to me: "This is the third time *you* came here, Dr. Miller. The other two times, they didn't even bother to show up."

I sighed and shrugged my shoulders.

The motion was made, seconded, and unanimously approved. Pete Aleman said a few words thanking the Student Government for their generosity, and within moments the body had approved an allocation of $120,000 to buy new computers for the computer labs.

"I guess they're feeling generous today," whispered Cal sarcastically.

"Now, Mr. — I mean *Dr.* — Miller, you may address us," sneered Niecey. "You have sixty seconds to speak."

"Thank you," I replied, standing up. I then addressed everyone in the crowded room. "Last semester, with the approval of Charles Okeke, my department chair, I began organizing a trip to Europe for CCSN students. This trip is unique. Thanks to the generous assistance of U.S. Senator Harry Reid, I was able to organize a trip in which participants will take part in discussions with officials at most of the key political and economic institutions in Europe. Participating students will have the opportunity to earn four academic credits for going on this trip and completing additional course requirements." All eyes in the room were upon me, except for those of Niecey. She was staring at her watch.

"This trip," I continued, "has sparked a great deal of interest amongst leading politicians in the state of Nevada. Senator Mark James and Assemblywoman Barbara Cegasvske have written letters praising this program. Regent Steve Sisolak and chair of the Board of Regents Jill Derby have also praised this trip. Senator Ray Shaffer will be joining us as a participant on the trip. It troubled me greatly, however, when several bright CCSN students approached me, stating that they would like to go on this trip, but that the cost of the trip was beyond their means. After consultation with several ASCCSN senators and with Mr. Braxton —"

"Your time is up," blurted Niecey.

I remained standing. "Madam President," I said, trying to be as polite as possible, "this is the third time I've come here to address this body on this issue. This is the first time you've had a quorum. I have a few more things to say, and I'd really appreciate it if you'd be kind enough to give me another minute, so that I can complete my statement."

"We have a long agenda today," she replied icily, "and I can't give you any more time."

"Madam President," called a young male voice from across the room. It was Senator Maurice Norrise.

Niecey pretended not to notice.

"Madam President," he called again, louder this time. All eyes looked toward Maurice. "Madam President, I defer my time on this issue to Dr. Miller, so that he can complete his statement."

Niecey glared at Maurice, and then glanced at Braxton. The Student Government advisor's eyes appeared to be filled with rage. He sat still for a moment, and then gave a slight nod.

"You may continue," said Niecey at last.

I took a deep breath. "After consultation with several ASCCSN senators and with Mr. Braxton, I submitted a request that you provide funds for some needy students who otherwise would be unable to go on this trip." I glanced at the students crowded into the room. It was for them that I was doing this.

"I have consulted with both CCSN Vice President Arlie Stops and UCCSN Assistant General Counsel Kwasi Nyamekye regarding this funding request," I continued. "Each said that he thought that the trip was a great educational opportunity, and that the Student Government would be within its powers, were it to fund travel stipends for needy students."

I paused and looked at Braxton. He glared at me, and I glanced back down at my notes. "Since I submitted the request," I said, "I have consulted several times with Mr. Braxton to make sure that I was following the appropriate procedures. I've also discussed the matter on many occasions with Treasurer Dave Abramson. Dave advised me to advertise the travel stipends widely, urging students to submit applications, to be reviewed by a committee of faculty members. He, as well as President Ransey, Senator Jose Lopez, and Mr. Braxton, advised me that it was appropriate for students to lobby you in favor of this proposal. I duly informed students in my department about this issue, and according to Dave, some sixty or seventy students have called or written to you in favor of funding this request." At that point a chorus of whispers erupted. My students smiled and whispered back and forth about their lobbying efforts, while the student senators murmured about the volume of calls and letters that they had received.

I cleared my throat, and the whispers died down. "I sent an e-mail to all faculty on March 15, asking them to urge their students to apply. I received dozens of requests for applications, and eight students had applied by the scheduled meeting of the faculty committee charged with reviewing the applications. Philosophy Instructor Mark Rauls and Political Science Professor Guillermo Monkman reviewed the applications. They rank-ordered the applicants, and requested that $20,955 be allocated for travel stipends. Since then, one applicant has withdrawn her application, due to a family responsibility. Furthermore, as I promised, I'll arrange for one student to travel for free. Therefore, I amend the request to $15,956." Several members of the student government jotted the figure down.

"The deadline for receipt of payment for this trip is Monday, April 12," I explained. "I request that you also allocate $95 per person, since Dave has told me you will be unable to provide checks by that date. This late fee is due to the fact that you did not have a quorum at your meeting two weeks ago and could not act on this request. Please do not penalize the students for this." I glanced at Dave Abramson, but he looked away.

"As promised," I continued, "I will arrange for one student to travel for free. So you only must allocate money for the other six. The total amount of money I am requesting, including the cost of the late fees, is $16,526." I noticed members of the student government crossing out what I assumed to be the old figure and jotting down the new one.

"I wish to thank the Student Government," I said in closing, "for considering providing the funds to make it possible for needy CCSN students to participate in this historic trip."

Niecey now gave the assembled students the opportunity to comment on my proposal to the Student Government. One-by-one the students spoke about how much they appreciated the hard work I had put into planning this trip and how much they expected to learn by going on the trip. Finally, Niecey recognized Nathan.

"My name is Nathan Taylor,"he said. "I'm a student at CCSN and also Senator Mark James' District Office Manager. I'm here to ask for your support on a very important opportunity for students at CCSN. Dr. Lee Miller has spent a lot of time arranging for a very educational trip to Europe. It's extraordinary how this CCSN instructor has gone above and beyond the call of duty to provide students with this great educational opportunity."

"Right on!" whispered Cal. Niecey glanced up from her watch just long enough to glare at us for a moment.

"This trip would give students first-hand knowledge of how European governments work," continued Nathan. "Students rarely have these kinds of opportunities and it would be a shame not to send as many students as possible. CCSN is known for championing new ideas and ways of making higher education more affordable as well as educationally rewarding; this is a chance to continue that tradition."

Several of the student senators nodded in agreement. Nathan smiled.

"I'm asking you to supply the funding to send as many students on this trip as possible," continued Nathan. "Myself — as well as State Senator Mark James — we're very supportive of the efforts of —"

"Your time is up!" announced Niecey.

Nathan looked like he was ready to bite her head off.

"Madam President!" blurted Maurice. "Madam President, I defer my time to this gentleman."

"Thanks," said Nathan to Maurice. He continued, addressing the rest of the people in the room. "I also want to let you know that when I called up and spoke to your president" — he gestured toward Niecey — "to show my support for this project, she was really rude to me on the phone. She said that it was none of my business whether or not she or anyone else supports this. I'm a student here, and she's been elected to represent students like me! When things started getting out of hand on the phone, she put Mr. Braxton on the line." Nathan gestured toward the Student Government advisor, whose eyes appeared to be ablaze. Nathan continued. "He chewed me out and said that this project was a bad idea and that there was no way he was going to let it pass."

"I don't know who you are! I never spoke to you!" yelled Braxton, shaking with rage.

"I don't know how you could forget me, sir, after the way you spoke to me on the phone!"

"I never spoke to you! I never said anything like that! Are you calling me a liar?"

"If that's what you contend, then yes, I'm calling you a liar. And I'm also telling you to your face that it's not your job to decide which projects the Student Government approves, and which they don't. That's for our elected representatives to decide!"

Nathan sat down. Braxton was so angry that he looked like he would explode at any second.

At that moment, Dave Abramson raised his voice. "Madam President, I'm ready to call the question, with the following amendment. I want to make sure that we don't get into trouble again with the Regents by funding this project. So I propose an amendment to the motion. We'll approve the funding request, but the money won't be disbursed until Dr. Miller gets it in writing from the chair of the Board of Regents and from the system attorney that there are no legal problems with us doing this."

Maurice seconded the motion, and the body approved the amendment. A few moments later, the Student Government — with only one dissenting vote — approved the travel stipend request.

Niecey moved on to the next item on the agenda without even taking a breath. I rose, and the students who had spoken in support of my request followed me out of the room.

"Congratulations!" I said to them. "You won! You're going to visit the European Union!"

"Thanks for fighting for us," said Cal. The other students echoed his sentiments.

I thanked them all for coming, especially Mark and Nathan, who had not even applied to go on the trip. Then I went back to my office, and breathed a sigh of relief.

I called up Jill Derby, chair of the Board of Regents. "I'm Lee Miller," I said, "political science instructor at CCSN. I'm calling you on a matter related to a trip to Europe that I had organized."

"Oh, yes," said Derby. "I got your letter. It sounds like a great trip. Too bad that I have some prior commitments."

"Thanks," I replied. "I've worked really hard on this. Anyway, the reason I'm calling is this. There were several students who wanted to go on this trip, but couldn't afford it. I asked the Student Government here at CCSN to allocate some money to help them out. They were concerned, though, that you might have some problems with them spending money in this way, or that there might be some legal problems. So they approved the money with the stipulation that I contact you and the UCCSN General Counsel to make sure that you have no objections."

"I don't know why they're asking for my opinion," said Derby. "They can spend their money however they want, unless there's some legal issue preventing it. Why don't you just fax the information on to Tom Ray, the General Counsel. If he says it's okay, then I'm fine with it."

"Great," I said. "I'll fax the information to Tom Ray. Thanks a lot."

I faxed the materials to General Counsel. I wanted to make sure that no one felt like s/he was being kept out of the loop, and my cc list was getting very long: Jill Derby, Steve Sisolak, Bob Silverman, Charles Okeke, and Kwasi Nyamekye. The fax machine was red-hot by the time I finished. Then I breathed a sigh of relief and went home for the night.

The next morning, Saturday, April 10, was the New Faculty Brunch. At 10:00 a.m. several dozen faculty members hired during the past two semesters assembled at the Las Vegas Country Club. The event was held in an elegant rotunda overlooking the beautifully manicured grounds and a sparkling lake. After enjoying a large buffet brunch, CCSN President Richard Moore rose to speak.

Moore had continued to be a very controversial figure since I had arrived in Las Vegas a year and a half earlier. He was famous for his success at currying favor with powerful politicians, and enlisting their support for many of his endeavors at CCSN. But Mike Green, Billy Monkman, and many other liberal faculty members had criticized him as tactless and politically biased when he had invited Kenny Guinn, the presumed Republican nominee for governor, to be graduation speaker the previous May. When Moore had named a building after Bill Raggio, the powerful Republican state senate majority leader from northern Nevada, local Democratic politicians denounced him, rightly pointing out that Raggio had been responsible for funneling disproportionate funding to northern Nevada colleges, at the expense of CCSN and UNLV. Moore also had spent over $100,000 purchasing equipment to create bronze busts of Guinn and Raggio, according to newspaper reports.[1] Furthermore, many people felt that Moore's marketing efforts were in bad taste: Moore had rented a billboard next to the McDonald's restaurant near the Charleston campus, reading, "Ten billion served — how to avoid a life of serving them — Community College of Southern Nevada."[2]

Nevertheless, Moore was charming, charismatic, and a good speaker — all valuable qualities for a college president. I have tried to recount what he said on this occasion as faithfully as my notes and my memory permit.

"I'm really glad you're all here," said Moore. "I always enjoy the opportunity to tell people how great CCSN is."

The crowd began to chuckle.

"But first," continued Moore, "I'd like to tell you about one recent achievement that I'm really proud about. When I got here at CCSN, I couldn't believe that a college of this stature had no sports teams. We now have big plans to introduce lots of sports at CCSN — baseball, soccer, and, uh… and lots of others. I'm sure you noticed this cap I'm wearing." Moore pulled the blue and gold baseball cap from his head and waved it to and fro for the crowd to see. "I'm really proud to announce that the new baseball team has finally begun practice. It took a lot of work, but they're up and running. This has been one of my favorite projects. I even got the school colors changed, so that they would match Berkeley, my alma mater." Moore replaced the cap on his head.

"Southern Nevada is a great place," continued Moore. "I want you all to get into the spirit of the place. You know, cowboy boots and all that. I've really developed an appreciation for bolo ties."

Several people chuckled at the thought of the CCSN president coming to work wearing cowboy boots and a bolo tie. Moore smiled. "Southern Nevada has got to be a great place if 6,000 people are moving here each month. But all those new people mean that there's room for lots of innovation, and lots of new ideas. Take our great new governor, Kenny Guinn. A lot of people said that Republicans don't care about education. Boy, did he prove them wrong! His Millennium Scholarships are going to make it possible for thousands more kids to go to college than ever before. Anyone with a "B" average gets a scholarship. What an idea!

"I know that some people criticized the scheme," Moore continued, "claiming that we're not going to have enough space here at CCSN for all those new students, with our budget as tight as it is. But this is part of the governor's secret plan. It's a Trojan horse to attack budget limitations. The governor knows that we're going to need a lot of money to expand our colleges to meet the surge in enrollment. He knows that this is the way he's finally going to be able to get a tax increase passed by the legislature. It's a brilliant plan!"

My jaw dropped in astonishment. "Mike Green was right," I thought to myself. "This guy *is* crazy if he thinks that a Republican governor has a secret plan to raise taxes!"

"Anyway," continued Moore, "I'm here to welcome you all to CCSN. Since I took over running this college four years ago, I've tried to instill in everyone our new motto, 'creating opportunities, changing lives.' I take this really seriously. I'm trying to build an institution that breaks all the rules. We need to reinvent education, to innovate, to try new things. And Bob here" — he gestured toward Silverman — "Bob has told me that you're all really impressive people who will contribute a lot to this college. So I'm offering you this challenge: don't be afraid to take risks. Try new things, and work as hard as you can to create more opportunities for your students, and to change their lives."

There was a big round of applause. Moore smiled and held up his hands. "Thank you," he said. "But now it's time for you to talk, and for me to listen. So this is what we're going to do. We'll go around the room, and I want each of you to introduce yourself, tell us your name and where you're from, and then tell us what you like about living in southern Nevada, and what you like about teaching at CCSN."

One by one the new faculty members spoke. I only half-listened. I was too busy thinking about what I would say. I had a sense that this was a pivotal moment for me. I had taken risks and tried new things to create opportunities for my students, just as Moore had urged us all to do. I realized that this was probably going to be my only chance to tell Moore in person that I was inspired by the same vision. I thought long and hard about what I was going to say. Finally my turn came.

"My name is Lee Miller," I said, scanning the faces in the crowd. "I got my Ph.D. at UCLA, and I taught for a while at UCLA and at a couple of colleges in Tokyo, Japan before coming to CCSN." I heard some murmurs in the audience. People were impressed with my credentials. Most of the speakers who had preceded me had only masters degrees — not Ph.D.s — and their degrees came from institutions less well-known than UCLA.

I grinned awkwardly, embarrassed, and continued. "What do I like about Nevada? As a political science instructor, what I like the most is how accessible the politicians are here. If I was still in California, there's no way that a U.S. senator would come to talk to my classes. But not in Nevada. Senator Reid came *twice* to speak to my students this year. That's one of the great things about living here in Nevada."

The audience was paying close attention, but I hardly noticed. By this point, my heart was racing. "What do I like about teaching at CCSN? The thing I like the most is the way that President Moore encourages us faculty to try new things. I took this to heart, and with the help of Senator Reid, I organized a trip to Europe for this summer. Students on this trip are going to meet with officials from the European Union, NATO, and other important institutions. They're going to learn first-hand about European politics."

President Moore shifted his weight, catching my eye. He was leaning forward, listening intently. That made me nervous. I shifted my gaze to the faculty members in the audience, and continued. "When some students were having trouble coming up with enough money to pay the cost of the trip, I tried an innovative approach. I asked the CCSN Student Government to help out by providing some funds. Just yesterday they approved the money, and now a bunch of needy students can go on this trip. One of them is a young woman named Razije. She's an Albanian from Yugoslavia, and she's really looking forward to our visit to the Yugoslav War Crimes Tribunal." The war in Kosovo, sparked by Yugoslav atrocities against ethnic Albanians, had just ended. There is a big airforce base just outside Las Vegas, and the airmen stationed there had played a major role in the Kosovo conflict.

"So, what do I like about CCSN?" I asked in closing. "What I like the most is that President Moore has created an environment that encouraged me to try all these new things."

The room erupted with cheers and thunderous applause. I blushed and walked toward my seat. Across the room, I noticed that Silverman's face had turned beet red.

As people were leaving, several congratulated me on the great work I had done. Then Silverman came up to me. "This has gone much too far!" he hissed. "Jill Derby called me up last night and chewed me out for an hour and a half! I thought I told you to come and meet with me!"

"I called JoAnn three times to make an appointment," I explained. "She kept putting me off."

"You'd better be at my office first thing on Monday morning!" snarled Silverman. Then he stomped off.

As I headed home, I was filled with foreboding. "Why is Silverman so angry with me?" I wondered. "Is he going to fire me? What have I done wrong?"

I decided that I'd better try to get things sorted out with Charles before Monday morning. I had been really upset by his e-mail canceling my political internship program, and by his refusal to come to my meeting with Silverman. But if I was finally going to face Silverman's wrath on Monday, I really needed to have my department chair by my side.

I called up Charles at home. "I read your e-mail," I said, trying like hell to keep my voice steady and calm.

"Yes," he replied, without emotion.

"I don't understand it at all," I said. "From the beginning you were very supportive of the European course. What's going on?" I noticed that my hands were shaking.

"I supported the idea of the trip and the course. But you never discussed the scholarship scheme with me."

"It never occurred to me to mention it to you, Charles," I replied. The pitch of my voice began to rise, as it does when I get upset. "I was just trying to work out a way for students to go, students who otherwise couldn't afford it. It had nothing to do with academics."

"But you used department letterhead in your letters about the scholarship scheme to various people. By doing so, you implicated me and the department in this thing."

I was dumbfounded. Everything I wrote in the context of my job went on department letterhead. I didn't know how to respond to

Charles' accusation. So I took a deep breath and decided to try tackling the internship issue first, and then come back to the meeting with Silverman.

"I'm really sorry about that," I said. "But in the same e-mail, you said you're canceling the internship course. I don't understand this. I got a grant for this program. You gave your approval for it. Students have actually begun their internships. If you cancel it now, they won't get credit. This is unfair to the students."

Charles exploded. "The class is cancelled! I've taken enough flak about your activities already! I want nothing to do with your internship class or your European trip or anything else that you do!" He hung up the phone.

I sat dumbfounded, the receiver dangling from my shaking hand until it fell onto my desk. "I can't believe this," I muttered. "None of this makes any sense."

I called up Mike Green. He listened patiently to my story and then, uncharacteristically, he exploded. "Charles should be standing up for you! That's a load of BS about using letterhead. I suppose that whenever I write a letter of recommendation for a student, I should use my personal stationery, or Charles will feel that the department as a whole is recommending the student!"

"I don't know what to do, Mike," I moaned. "I can't figure out what's going on. It's like I'm in the Twilight Zone, or something."

"Welcome to CCSN," he muttered, cynically. "Moore is a raving lunatic, and everyone who works for him is following in his footsteps. When they say you've got to be crazy to work for that guy, they aren't kidding. Now, listen to me. Go in and meet with Silverman. Sit there and listen to him rant and rave, and don't interrupt, don't disagree with him, don't try to defend yourself, just sit there and nod your head. Eventually, the guy will run out of steam. Then play the nice little boy and say you're sorry and that it won't happen again. Then leave his office and go back to doing exactly what you were doing before. Clearly, this is just a case of some fat administrator looking for a punching bag for his frustrations. You've done nothing wrong."

"But Silverman says he's getting flak over this from Jill Derby, the chair of the Board of Regents." I related the details to him.

"I wouldn't worry too much about Derby," said Mike. "I find it pretty hard to believe that she's behind this. There's nothing at stake here that would matter system-wide."

"But what about Al Balboni? He's pissed off at me because Silverman thinks he officially endorsed my funding request. Dave Abramson had asked me to ask Al for his endorsement. I told Dave that Al wouldn't take a position on it, because he felt that it compromised the integrity of his position as chair of the Faculty Senate. But Dave must be telling people otherwise."

"Integrity!" Mike chuckled cynically. "Balboni is a former administrator. He doesn't seem to think that Silverman could lie." Mike sighed. "But don't worry about Al. I'll talk to him. Just 'yes' Silverman to death until this thing blows over."

"Thanks, Mike," I said. "I feel a lot better." I was lying. I was very nervous.

"Go get 'em," he said.

Next I called up Linda Foreman. She said that she could not come to Silverman's office on the West Charleston campus on Monday morning, since her classes were across town at the Cheyenne campus. But she promised to take part in the discussion via speaker-phone.

The next day, I called Steve Sisolak, and told him what had transpired at the New Faculty Brunch. "Silverman said that Jill Derby had called him up and chewed him out for an hour and a half on Friday night."

"This doesn't make any sense," said Steve. "I'll tell you what. I'm scheduled to talk with Jill this afternoon. I'll ask her about this, and then call you back."

I thanked Steve, and waited impatiently for several hours. Finally, the phone rang.

"Jill said that she spoke with Bob," said Steve, "But she denied chewing him out. She said that it was Bob who was upset. She said Bob told her that you hadn't gone through the proper chain of command, and that you'd refused to meet with him."

"That's ridiculous!" I replied. "I've been trying for weeks to get an appointment, but his secretary keeps telling me that he's too busy."

"Well, that's what Jill told me. She said that Bob had problems with two issues: process and the amount of money. Jill said that she thinks that the Student Government can pretty much spend their money however they want. In terms of 'process,' Jill said that she just hopes that you and Bob can work through whatever concerns he has."

"That's pretty much what she told me when I spoke with her on Friday," I said.

"Yes, she mentioned that you called. She told me that she doesn't want to get involved in this thing, but that she will read the report prepared by the General Counsel's Office."

"Well, that's good news. Silverman made it sound like she was pressuring him to put a stop to it. Maybe she could write a letter stating that it isn't for the Regents to decide how the Student Government spends their money, so long as there are no legal problems."

"That's not a bad idea," Steve replied.

IX

A Crime Against the Bureaucracy

I spent the rest of the weekend worrying about the meeting. Then, on the morning of Monday, April 12, I met Dr. Silverman in his office. Marion "Page" Littlepage, dean of curriculum and scheduling, was there. I felt quite alone, despite the fact that Linda Foreman, the NFA president, was on the speaker-phone.

"You're in a lot of trouble, Lee," said Silverman. His voice was even, but it was clear that he was struggling to contain his rage. "To start off, I'm going to give you some coaching about how to proceed in this conversation. It is time for you to listen, not to talk. Your problem thus far is that you haven't been listening."

I squirmed under Silverman's glare, but I held my tongue.

"You're a first-year instructor. It seems like you've forgotten that. You've managed to piss off the four people who are most critical to your career: Al Balboni and Candace Kant, the Faculty Senate chairs, Charles Okeke, your department chair, and me. Without us on your side, there's no way you're going to get tenure, or even keep your job at all, for that matter. Your own department chair refused to come to this meeting! You're not following the chain of command. You're not keeping us in the loop. Al and Candace were so angry that they wrote to me to complain. They said that you'd been lying to them, and that there's no way they're going to support you when it comes to your tenure."

I was shocked. I could not believe that Al and Candace had said such things. But I remembered Mike's advice, and I kept silent.

"That was quite a stunt you pulled at the brunch. You were trying to go over my head to Richard Moore. Well, Richard knows all about what you've been up to. He made it clear to me that he won't put up with it. I have his full support on this."

I shuddered. "At the brunch I just said that Dr. Moore inspired me to be innovative. I don't understand."

"Don't play dumb with me. You were trying to make a fool out of me at that meeting! Don't play that game. You may get hurt." Silverman glared at me, and I averted my eyes.

Silverman shifted his weight in his chair. "You're not keeping me in the loop. Why do I have to hear everything through the grapevine?" Silverman's voice began to rise in anger. "Do you know that it was Dave Abramson who told me about this thing! Why do I have to hear about it from a student? He told me that he thought these scholarships were a terrible idea, that he opposed them, that he would make sure that they don't pass."

"That deceitful son of a bitch!" I thought. If what Silverman said was true, Abramson had set me up. He had been urging me on, and at the same time undermining my position with Silverman when he and the college vice president had met to discuss the Student Government budget.

"And now," continued Silverman, "I hear that you've been talking behind my back to Steve Sisolak. Al is convinced that you badmouthed him to Sisolak, and he plans to call the guy up and set him straight."

Silverman's face began to redden. "You think you're so important. You have friends in high places. You speak to people like Sisolak, Jill Derby, and Shelley Berkley. You're a friend of Harry Reid. Well, I've got news for you. I speak to Harry Reid too. When I call him up, he returns my phone calls! I'm sure you've been badmouthing me to him, and after I get through with you, I'm going to call him up and set him straight!"

Silverman was shaking with rage. He took a deep breath, trying to calm himself. "You've been doing an end-run around process. Your chair won't even come to this meeting. Well, I'm here to coach you. You've made every conceivable mistake. You think you're an agent of change like Richard. Well, you're not. You're nothing! You're just a first-year instructor!"

I trembled in the face of this huge man's fury. I was simultaneously scared and angry and confused. I could think of no logical reason why Moore and Silverman would be mad that I had taken Moore at his word and tried to be innovative, tried to create opportunities for my students. Was Moore angry that I was stealing his thunder? It was terribly unjust.

Silverman continued to harangue me. "You haven't been following the process. You need to speak to Page to get your course in the schedule. You need to speak to Chemene Crawford about scholarships. You claim to be doing all this for the students, but you come across as self-serving. I know very well that you need 16 students to get full pay for teaching this course. These scholarships are just a way for you to meet that threshold."

I gasped. "They think I'm doing this for the money!" I thought, burning with righteous indignation. "They're insane! I've spent so many hours trying to get these damned scholarships for my students that I would have been a lot better off moonlighting at McDonald's!"

Silverman stopped screaming at me and turned to Page. "Is there any precedent for this?"

Page stroked his mustache. "Well, last year, Elfie took a group of students to Europe, and the Student Government kicked in some money. But she went about it differently. She had the students set up a club, and they applied for the money. She didn't apply for it herself."

"Do you want me to ask the students to set up a club?" I asked meekly.

"Don't be ridiculous!" roared Silverman. "It's much too late for that." He shook his head at me. "Rather than following the process in place, you create your own procedures. You set up your own selection criteria. Someone who doesn't get selected can sue, charging discrimination."

"But only eight people applied, and the selection committee recommended that all of them be funded!" I blurted.

"This isn't a matter for some committee *you* set up!" roared Silverman. "This is a matter for Chemene, for Financial Aid!"

"But I tried to speak to Chemene Crawford, like you asked me to," I gasped. "She was out of town, so I figured that I should speak to her boss. Arlie Stops told me that the students can't get additional financial aid to go on this trip, and that going to the Student Government was the right thing to do."

"Arlie Stops has *less* than no credibility with me! He has negative credibility!"

My jaw dropped. I could not believe that he was insulting a fellow vice president in front of me.

"I should pull the plug on this thing!" thundered Silverman. "You're establishing a dangerous precedent. Everyone knows this. No one even wants to talk to you anymore! Not Al, not Candace, not even Charles, your own department chair!"

"But I don't understand this," I pleaded. "I discussed this trip in the beginning with Charles and with Al. They were very supportive from day one."

"They tell me that you were not being honest with them! You're in big trouble. You didn't follow procedures!"

"What procedures was I supposed to follow? I discussed everything with Al and with Charles before I did anything. Charles approved the class. When I asked the Student Government for money, I followed the procedures there. What other procedures was I supposed to follow?"

At this point Linda finally spoke up. "Bob, we have no procedures for study abroad. That's why I held that forum at the beginning of the semester."

"Then we'd better set some up!" snapped Silverman, furious that Linda had revealed the absurdity of his accusations against me.

Silverman turned back to me. "Why did you bring Jill Derby into this?" he demanded. "She chewed me out on the phone for an hour and a half on Friday night!"

"I had to call her," I explained, my voice quaking. "When the Student Government approved the funding, the motion required me to contact her and Tom Ray to make sure they didn't have any problems with it."

"So, now you're taking orders from the Student Government?" he asked sarcastically. "No, you take orders from *me*! I'm your boss, not a group of students!" This time I took Mike's advice and kept my mouth shut. Silverman seemed to have lost his mind.

He turned to Page. "If you were me, what would you do?"

Page sighed. "I'd pull the plug on this."

Silverman scratched his head, and was silent for a few moments. His rage suddenly seemed to dissipate, like a morning fog. "No, I don't think I'm going to do that," he said slowly, as if a new thought had just occurred to him. "No. This project is a good one. He's made a lot of mistakes. But I think he's salvageable." Silverman turned to me. "Lee, creativity and innovation aren't enough," he said, no longer screaming, but instead speaking to me like a loving father reprimanding a naughty child. "You need to follow procedures. I think you're salvageable. You need some coaching, but I think we can keep you for now. You'd just better make sure to let me know about everything that you do in the future."

"I'll make sure," I said sheepishly. I felt angry and humiliated, but I was thankful that Silverman had stopped screaming at me. I decided to play the apologetic child, as Mike had advised.

"Good," said Silverman. He gave me a tired grin, as if to indicate that he was glad that he had finally gotten through to his stubborn son. "I want you to go and get Charles and bring him over to Page's office. I want the three of you to get that class into the schedule for summer."

I nodded and opened my mouth to respond. But Silverman held up his hand. "One more thing. Natalie Patton had better not get wind of this."

My eyes opened wide for just a moment, before I forced myself to hide my astonishment. Natalie Patton was the reporter who had exposed the scandal surrounding the international student recruitment efforts of Bill Cassell. I noted that Silverman seemed to be afraid of her. I nodded in agreement. "Thanks," I said.

Silverman dismissed me. I hurried back to the PRS department office and located Charles. He seemed to bristle when he saw me.

"I met with Dr. Silverman," I said, ignoring Charles' coldness, "and we got this thing all straightened out. He gave the go-ahead for the European trip, and he wants you and me to go over to Page's office to get the scheduling issues worked out."

Charles' tension seemed to melt away as I uttered these words. "I'm very glad to hear that," he said.

Charles did not ask any questions about the meeting. He no longer seemed to be hostile, and I didn't want to mess things up. If I started talking about the meeting, I feared that I would blurt out how upset I was about his refusal to go and back me up. So I held my tongue during the short walk to Page's office.

Page had beaten us there. He and Charles both signed a form placing in the summer schedule the course associated with my European trip.

"Thanks a lot," I said to Charles as we walked back to the department office. I was very relieved that things were back on track.

"I'm very happy to know that everything turned out okay," he replied. The distance between us seemed to have evaporated. I felt like it was a good time to clear up something that was bothering me.

"Charles," I said, "Dr. Silverman said that you had told him you were mad at me, and that you would be reluctant to support my tenure application down the road."

Charles stopped in his tracks. He stood there silently for several seconds, as if in shock. Then he shook his head. "I don't know what he's talking about," said Charles. "I said no such thing."

Of all Silverman's rantings, his assertion that all my colleagues had turned against me was by far the most painful. Now that Charles had denied it, I felt compelled to confront Al.

I returned to my office and called up Al Balboni on the phone. "Al," I said, "I met with Dr. Silverman about the scholarship thing. He chewed me out for half an hour nonstop, but ultimately, he gave the go-ahead for the trip and the associated course."

"Congratulations," said Al. The words were devoid of enthusiasm. I ignored his aloofness and pressed onward.

"There's one thing that Silverman told me, something that I'm concerned about. He said that you and Candace wrote him a letter criticizing me, and that you told him you would oppose me getting tenure."

There was silence at the other end of the line for quite a while. Finally, Al spoke. "I don't know where he got that from," said Al. He spoke slowly, as if he was choosing his words carefully. "I was angry when I found out that the scholarships had been cancelled, after I had gone to the trouble of urging my students to apply. But I never expressed to Dr. Silverman my dissatisfaction with you, and I never said that I would stand in the way of you getting tenure."

Al had been my mentor, and I had no reason to doubt his sincerity. I thanked him for clearing this up.

When I called up Candace a little later, she seemed genuinely annoyed at what Silverman had said. "I'm not mad at you for any reason," she declared. "I never spoke to Bob about you, and I can't believe that he would make up something like this!" Before hanging up, Candace announced her intention to give Silverman a piece of her mind.

I was very relieved. Silverman must have lied to me, I decided. My colleagues had not denounced me to him.

I stepped over to my mailbox and retrieved my mail. I flipped through the stack, finding the usual collection of advertisements for textbooks, and notices about events taking place on campus. Then I came across a copy of a memo, dated April 9, from Niecey to the Student Government. She had cc'd me. It read as follows:

> I hereby veto the action you took on Friday, April 9, 1999 when you authorized an appropriation that would allow students to travel to Europe as part of a Political Science class. I do so for three reasons.
>
> First, in my opinion, the decision as to which students would receive the benefit was made by three members of the faculty using an arbitrary and capricious selection process. Approximately 30,000 students attend the Community College of Southern Nevada. I am not convinced that only eight students desired to avail themselves of this opportunity.
>
> Second, in my opinion, even though the persons who determined the financial need were probably acting in good faith, the decision as to which students did or did not have financial need was made arbitrarily, and was not made using any recognized methodology that would support a fair or just determination.
>
> Third, in my opinion, the invoking of the names of a United States Senator, a Nevada State Senator, "other members of the Nevada Legislature," members of the UCCSN Regents, and the legal counsel for the UCCSN Regents and declaring that they supported and approved of this project brought unnecessary, undue and external pressure on the Student Government Senate that was inappropriate.

I was flabbergasted. I was shocked to learn that the Student Government president had veto power. I had believed that, once the Student Government had approved the funds, it was a done deal. What a shock! I felt like the wind had been knocked out of me.

I sent copies of the memo as a courtesy to Billy Monkman and Mark Rauls, the two professors who had served on the selection committee. Then I called up each of the applicants for the money and broke the news to them.

Several of them — good political science students that they were — asked me whether the student senate had the power to override Niecey's veto, like the U.S. Congress can override the president's veto. After all, the senate had been overwhelmingly in favor of the allocation. There had been only a single dissenting vote.

"I would think so," I answered my students hesitantly. "You should go down to the Student Government office and get a copy of their constitution to find out."

After I got off the phone, I e-mailed Bob Silverman. I had promised to keep him informed of all my activities in the context of the European trip:

Dear Dr. Silverman,

I met this afternoon with Page and with Charles. We were able to work out the curriculum and scheduling issues to everyone's satisfaction.

I also learned that Niecey Ransey, Student Government President, vetoed the travel stipend allocation that was approved by the Student Government last Friday. I understand that a veto can be overridden; the students who were recipients of stipends are in favor of attempting this.

Do you have any thoughts on this issue? I value your input/coaching.

Sincerely,

Lee Miller

I wasn't at all sure what Silverman had meant by "coaching," but I figured that I should express some enthusiasm for it, since he had stressed its necessity to me in our meeting.

Silverman wrote back to me the next day:

Thank you for this update. I'm glad Charles you and Page worked it out. Re veto I will inquire and let you know. I reviewed my E-mail and the one I thought came from Candace was not there so I must have made an error reading a cc insted [sic] of from [sic] I hope this helps to clear the air Bob

I made sure to call Candace to thank her for setting the record straight.

"I don't know anything about the problems you're having with Bob right now," she told me, "but there's no way I'm going to let him put words in my mouth."

I also called up Larry Tomlinson. Larry had been the chair of the search committee that had recommended me for my job at CCSN, and since then he had always lavished praise on me for my hard work. "Lee," he said, "I don't regret for a moment our decision to hire you. You've done a great job so far. But let me give you a piece of advice. I've been here at CCSN for twenty-some-odd years. The politics can get really nasty. Watch yourself in the future. For now, make sure to send a conciliatory memo to Charles and to Bob apologizing for this whole thing."

"Okay," I replied. "Thanks for the advice."

I was glad that Larry still supported me privately, but very disappointed that he didn't offer to do so publicly.

Next I called up Mike Green to let him know what had transpired. I was pretty sure that Mike already knew all the details. Somehow he always seemed to know everything about everyone. Nevertheless Mike patiently listened to my story. He was particularly interested in Silverman's assertion that Charles, Al, and Candace had told him that they were mad at me and would stand in the way of my tenure.

"Clearly someone is lying," observed Mike. "Based on experience, it's more likely to be Silverman, though anything is possible. On the other hand, I'm glad to hear that Candace had the backbone to tell Silverman off. Furthermore, I did happen to talk to Charles yesterday. He mentioned to me that you told him that Silverman said that he — Charles — would oppose your tenure. Charles told me that he was disturbed by Silverman putting words in his mouth, and that he'd made it a point to let Silverman know."

"I'm glad to hear that," I said, relieved. "I was on the verge of believing that Silverman was right, that everyone in the world was pissed off at me."

"Now, Lee, didn't I tell you always to operate from the assumption that everything an administrator tells you is a lie?"

I laughed.

"One more thing," said Mike. "I spoke to Gary Elliott last night, and filled him in on what had occurred." Gary Elliott was the former DEA agent turned history professor who was notorious for never attending department meetings. "Gary can always boil down stuff to what it really means. This was his observation: Lee, you have 'committed a crime against the bureaucracy.'"

I had a good laugh at that one. How true it was.

Later that day I was in the PRS department office. I noticed Mark Rauls and Jim Fuller pointing at a piece of paper and laughing derisively. Mark and Jim were among the junior faculty cadre who frequented Billy Monkman's parties, and Mark had served on the travel stipend selection committee. They called me over. "Arbitrary and capricious, eh?" cried Mark. "I bet she doesn't even know what 'arbitrary and capricious' means."

"I know for a fact that she doesn't," replied Jim. "She's in my class. I've read her papers. There's no way that Niecey Ransey wrote this memo. The next time she's in class — when that will be, I don't know, since she hardly ever shows up — the next time she's in class, right in the middle of my lecture, I'm going to stop mid-sentence, and point at her. 'Niecey,' I'm going to say, 'please define 'arbitrary and capricious.'"

The three of us laughed.

A few weeks later, on May 10, I spoke with a student whom I'll call Sally. Sally was a student at CCSN who was very excited about her plans to go on the European trip. She was very outspoken and pro-active, and had helped me to recruit other students to participate. Sally had not applied for a travel stipend from the student government, but she happened to know Niecey personally. Sally told me that Niecey had admitted to her that she had vetoed the money on the recommendation of Larry Braxton. "Hmm," I thought. "Perhaps Niecey had a ghost writer after all."

Later that day, I spoke to Cal Chadwick, the student who was coordinating the students' efforts to get the veto overridden. "I went over to the Student Government office today," he told me. "I spoke to Dave Abramson. Dave said that they will bring the motion up for an override next week. Niecey can veto it again if she wants, but at the following meeting she'll be out of office, and it'll be in the hands of the next Student Government. So, we should have this all sorted out within two more Student Government meetings, at the latest. Dave promised that the funding will be approved in the end, and that he'll make sure to cover any late fees."

"That's good to hear," I replied. "But I'm sorry that this is taking so long."

"Me too," said Cal. "But we'll keep at it. Oh, I forgot to tell you. While I was at the Student Government office, I picked up a copy of their constitution."

"Great. What did you find out about overriding vetoes?"

"That's the funny thing." He shook his head. "I couldn't find it. I looked really carefully. Then I noticed that every other page was missing."

"Why am I not surprised?"

Cal sighed. "I guess I'll have to go back and get another copy."

This week was the final stretch in the Student Government election campaign. Every time I entered the campus, I was handed dozens of flyers advertising various candidates. It was a bit of a nuisance, but I was happy to put up with it. It provided an extracurricular lesson in democracy for my students. In fact, I made it a point to invite the candidates to come to my classes to address my students and answer their questions. Several of them did so, including Dave Abramson.

"Niecey should never have vetoed the scholarships," declared Dave Abramson in front of my class. "If I'm elected president, the first thing I'll do is call an emergency meeting and get those funds approved. I'll get those checks ready, even if I have to write out all of them by hand!" He got a huge round of applause from my students.

On Friday, April 16, Dave Abramson was elected president of the Student Government by a landslide. A half-dozen of my students had run for various offices, and to my disappointment, not one of them was elected. But, based on Dave's campaign promises, I had reason to be optimistic that the Student Government would soon approve the travel stipends.

During the next week I put aside the distractions of the travel stipend affair, and concentrated on other matters. I had a huge stack of essays to grade. I was also busy making the preparations for a trip to Washington, D.C. I had been awarded a grant to spend a week shadowing Congresswoman Shelley Berkley. Berkley, a former regent, was the congressional candidate whom I had met a year and a half earlier, soon after I had arrived in Nevada, when she had hosted a reception in honor of Senator and Mrs. Reid. Berkley had won the election, and now represented southern Nevada in the U.S. House of Representatives. I looked forward to spending a week in Washington, following the congresswoman around from morning to night, learning first-hand what the job of a member of Congress entails.

On Thursday, April 22, I received a memo from Kwasi Nyamekye, the assistant general counsel for UCCSN whom I had spoken to on the phone before the previous Student Government meeting. Nyamekye was writing back on behalf of Tom Ray, in response to my letter asking for a legal opinion about whether the Student Government could fund the travel stipends. Kwasi wrote back that neither the Student Government nor I had the authority to request a legal opinion from the general counsel's office. Only the college president may do that, he explained. In other words, the Student Government is left to its own discretion, unless Richard Moore objects to the allocation. I let Dave Abramson know.

The following day was the next scheduled meeting of the Student Government. But no meeting was held. I called up Dave to find out why.

"Niecey never called a meeting," he explained. "In order for us to have a meeting, she needs to post an agenda which states the meeting date. She never posted anything, so we didn't meet."

"What? I thought you had regular meeting times."

"We do. Every other Friday. But we can't hold a scheduled meeting unless Niecey posts the agenda. Our next meeting will be her last. She has to pass the gavel to me. She must be stalling, so that we can't override her veto."

"So, when will your next meeting be?" I asked.

"Next Friday, hopefully," he replied. "I'll try to convince her to post the agenda. I know she's prepared one. Somehow we've got to get it on the bulletin board."

"Good luck," I said.

Each day during the following week I looked for the agenda, but it never appeared. On Friday, April 30, there was no Student Government meeting.

Cal and some of the other students waiting on the travel stipends were getting impatient. Several times since the veto they had gone down to the Student Government office to ask for copies of the constitution and related documents. Each time they were told that the documents were being revised, and that new copies would be available in a few days. I even went down there myself, and received the same response. All they could give me, they said, was a copy with every other page missing.

By Thursday, May 6, there still was no agenda posted. The students were very frustrated, as was I. But I had no idea what to do about the problem.

That morning I happened to call Tod Story, Congresswoman Berkley's local office manager, to finalize the arrangements for my upcoming trip to Washington. I had received word on May 3 that my grant for the trip had been approved. After we got the details straightened out, Tod asked me how things were going with my job at CCSN.

"My students are great," I said. "But I'm really frustrated about the way the Student Government president is stonewalling over a project I'm involved in. She vetoed the money that is supposed to send some of my students on a trip to the European Union. Now she refuses to hold another meeting, so that it's impossible for the senate to override her veto. My students and I have been trying to get a copy of the Student Government constitution for weeks, to try to find a way to get around this problem, but they won't give us one."

"That's totally illegal," said Tod. "I was involved in Student Government when I was at UNLV. Under the Nevada Open Records Law, you have to give out a copy of any public document within forty-eight hours of receiving a request."

Armed with this knowledge, I walked down to the Student Government office. I asked for a copy of the constitution, and again was told that no copies were available. When I insisted that they had to give me a copy under state law, they sent me to see Braxton.

"How can I help you, Lee?" said Braxton smirking. He seemed so much more cheerful this time, compared to the other times I had met him. I supposed that he was gloating over Niecey's veto.

"Larry, several of my students have been trying for weeks to get a copy of the Student Government constitution, to read up on the procedures for overriding a veto. Each time they were told that no copies were available."

"I can give you a copy of the Constitution, but not the by-laws and statutes. We made a lot of changes to them this year. I pulled all the copies. We haven't had the chance to enter the changes into the computer. We'll probably get to it over the summer."

"I really need a copy right now. Could I at least have a copy of the old version, please?"

"I have no intention of giving you a copy," said Braxton, smiling. "If you want one, you'll have to wait till mid-June."

I sighed, realizing that mid-June would be too late for the students who were counting on the travel stipends. I was sure that Braxton knew this as well. "Sorry," I said, "but I can't wait that long. I'm going to have to inform you that, under the Nevada Open Records Law, you must give me a copy of a public document within forty-eight hours of when I request it. I've been waiting more than three weeks."

"Why you —" began Braxton, his face flushed with what appeared to be rage. Then he checked himself. "Fine, within forty-eight hours," he hissed through gritted teeth.

Several years have now passed since that meeting with Braxton. I have yet to receive a copy of anything from him.

As I was walking back to my office, I ran into Dave Abramson. I told him that I was having a lot of trouble getting a copy of the Student Government constitution, by-laws, and statutes.

"I'll lend you my own copy," he said. "Do you have class tonight?"

"Yes, at 7:30–10:30. Same room as where you made your campaign speech."

"Great," said Dave. "I'll drop it off in your class."

When I got back to my office, I sent the following e-mail:

Dear Dr. Silverman,

As promised, I am writing to keep you informed of all my activities related to the Student Government Travel Stipend issue.

After the April 9 veto by President Ransey of the travel stipends, several of my students asked me questions about the procedures surrounding the vetoes, meetings, etc. I did not know the answers to their questions, and I suggested that they consult the ASCCSN Student Government Constitution, By-Laws, and Statutes. The students requested copies of these documents at the Student Government Office, and they were told that no copies were available.

My students then asked me if I might be able to get them copies. Several times over the past 3 weeks I have requested copies of these documents, so that I could provide the requested information, and each time I was always told that the documents were being revised, and that they would be available in a few days.

At one point I was given a copy of the documents that I requested, but every alternate page was missing. When I returned to the Student Government office to request a full copy, I was told that all copies on hand had every alternate page missing, and that full copies would be available in a few days. Upon subsequent requests, I was again [told] that the documents were being revised, and that they were unavailable.

Today I spoke to Larry Braxton, Student Government Advisor, and he told me that he could give me a copy of the Constitution, but that the By-Laws and Statutes were still being revised; he expected them to ready by mid-June.

I reminded Mr. Braxton that, under the Nevada Open Records Law, public documents must be made available within 48 hours of request. He told me that he would make sure to have copies available within 48 hours.

Thanks again for your interest in my endeavors.

Sincerely,

Lee Miller

At 7:30 that evening I was standing in front of my class, taking roll. Dave Abramson entered the room and lumbered up to my lectern. He handed me a thick stack of papers held together by a binder clip. The students in the class stopped their chatter.

"Ah, at last," I said. "Thanks."

"Sorry it took so long," he replied.

I flipped through the constitution, and came to Article V, Executive Board and Senate Meetings. "Hey, Dave, it says here that the senate must meet a minimum of twice a month. You only met once last month — the meeting at which you passed the funding for the scholarships. Niecey can't refuse to hold meetings. It violates your constitution."

"There's nothing I can do about it," said Dave defensively. He backed toward the door. "I can't call a meeting until I assume the presidency. Niecey needs to call the meeting."

"Look, we both know that she's stalling so that her veto won't be overridden until it's too late for the scholarship students to go on the trip. You're an officer in the Student Government. If the president is violating the constitution, I'd say it's your duty to set things right. If she doesn't want to call a meeting, then perhaps *you* should!"

"Okay," said Dave, heading for the door. "Tomorrow morning, before 11:00, I'll be in my office. Send a couple of your students down to speak to me, and I'll consider calling a meeting myself for tomorrow afternoon." Dave hurriedly departed.

After the class was over, I spoke to Cal Chadwick. "Niecey's actions are totally unconstitutional," I said.

"What can we do?" he asked.

"I'm heading back to my office. I'll take a careful look at the constitution and by-laws, and then let you know. Can I fax you something tonight?"

"Sure," said Cal. "I'll be waiting."

Half an hour later, I faxed him the following:

Despite what we were told by members of the Student Government, the Student Government can, and indeed must, meet even if the President does not want it to.

The Constitution takes precedence over the By-Laws and Statutes. It is the duty of members of the Student Government to uphold the Constitution. In the event that the By-Laws or Statutes conflict with the Constitution, they must act to uphold the Constitution.

Constitution, sec. 005.000 states the following:

The Senate shall determine, at the first regularly scheduled meeting of the semester, the days, times and locations of subsequent meetings for that semester. Posters announcing changes must be displayed at each of the campuses and extension centers.

The Student Government is in violation of this provision. They voted to make their regularly scheduled meeting every other Friday at 3 p.m. Their last regularly scheduled meeting was April 9. They did not hold their regularly scheduled meeting on April 23. Nor did they put up posters announcing any changes.

Their next regularly scheduled meeting is May 7. If this meeting is not held, they will be in violation of the Constitution.

I can locate no Statute or By-Law stating that only the President may call a meeting. Even if such a provision were to exist, it would violate the Constitutional requirement that meetings be held at the scheduled times. The Constitution takes precedence over conflicting Statutes and By-Laws.

Constitution, sec. 005.005: "The ASCCSN Senate shall meet in open meetings at a minimum of two (2) times monthly for conducting business."

They only met once last month, in violation of their Constitution.

Constitution, sec. 005.006: "Permanent posters announcing days, times and locations of meetings will be prominently displayed at all campuses and extension centers."

No such posters exist, in violation of the Constitution.

It is my opinion that a Student Government meeting must be held on May 7, regardless of the opinion of the President, if the provisions of the Constitution are to be satisfied.

David Abramson, current Treasurer, and President-elect, said in your presence that he will call a meeting tomorrow, as is required by the Constitution, provided that you and at least one other student meet with him tomorrow morning at his office before 11 a.m. to urge him to do so. It would be in your best interest to meet with him, as he requested.

The Student Government answers directly to the Regents. Regent Steve Sisolak has been very supportive of this endeavor. It might be beneficial if you were to inform him of the information above. President Ransey has been stalling in an unconstitutional manner to deprive you and others of the opportunity to go on this trip.

I gave Cal Steve Sisolak's phone number, as well as that of Nathan Taylor, Senator James' district manager. I also urged him to contact the other students, to see if they could go with him to meet with Dave Abramson. I even gave him my own home phone number, and asked him to give me a call in the morning, to let me know what transpired at the meeting. Then I went home for the night.

The next day, Cal let me know that, given the short notice, none of the other students were able to go with him. So he met with Dave alone. Dave refused to call a meeting for that afternoon, arguing that it would do no good anyway because, without more notice, they could not expect a quorum. But Dave promised Cal to do what he could to get a Student Government meeting scheduled for the following Friday, May 14.

After class the following Wednesday, May 12, Cal told me that he'd met again with Dave Abramson. Dave told him that Niecey had finally agreed to call a meeting. It was scheduled for the afternoon of May 19.

"Congratulations," I replied. "I hope you can get this all straightened out. Unfortunately, at that time I'll be on a plane to Washington. I'll be spending a week learning about Congress with Congresswoman Berkley."

"Do you think that they scheduled it at that time so that you wouldn't be able to come?"

I just shrugged my shoulders. I figured that he was probably right, but there was nothing that I could do about it.

Mike Green graciously agreed to be point-man on the European trip while I was out of town. I gave him the phone numbers for the tour company, as well as the numbers for all the people who had signed up for the trip, including the scholarship students.

On Saturday, May 15, while I grading finals, the phone rang. It was Gertrude. She was very upset.

"They fired me from my job!" she cried. "My boss in the Counseling Department fired me, and said that I was banned from campus! I asked him why, and he said that he didn't know, but that Silverman had told him 'to get me out *now*!' The other counselors were in tears. They pleaded with him, telling him that I was diligent and reliable and that no one had ever complained about me. But my boss said that it was out of his hands, that he was only carrying out Silverman's orders. I'm graduating in a week. They had offered me a full-time job in the counseling department after graduation. I've only just been able to pay the rent with my Social Security and this work

129

study job. I'm a sixty-eight-year-old lady. I haven't hurt anyone. Why are they doing this to me? They won't even tell me!"

I tried to comfort Gertrude. I felt terrible for her. I asked her if she could think of anything she had done to get Silverman angry with her.

"I've never even met the man!" she cried. "I'm just a part-time student employee here. Why would the senior vice president take any notice of me? I get along great with all the administrators I know. Especially Arlie Stops — he's been my mentor. The only time I can think of that I had an argument with an administrator at CCSN was the time I chewed out Larry Braxton, that rude man who's the Student Government advisor."

"Oh my God," I thought. "First they went after me. Now they're going after the students."

I was powerless to do anything to help Gertrude. I could only offer her words of comfort and support. Gertrude said that she planned to go see Silverman and find out why he had ordered her fired. I suggested that she bring someone along with her as a witness. I also urged her to contact Arlie Stops, to see if he could be of assistance.

Over the next few days, I frantically tried to complete my grading. Quite a few students had submitted extra credit reports about politically-oriented activities that they had taken part in, such as volunteer work or even running for Student Government. One of these reports came from Mark Leichty. It read, in part, as follows:

> When I first started campaigning, I had no idea of how incompetent and crooked the Student Government members were.... My opponent for the presidency was Dave Abramson. He was current treasurer at the time of the elections and he recruited just about everyone running for a position to run against me....
>
> [W]hen the fliers for all the candidates were posted, mine was not. When I went to talk to Braxton about this problem of when my flier was to be posted, he didn't give me straight answers to when it was to be posted.
>
> ...There was an assembly for a pre-election "meet the candidates" debate that was held in the student lounge. When I arrived, Dave was on the stage talking about me and started to yell when he saw me enter.
>
> ... I [had] consulted former members of the Student Government that had worked with him in the past that didn't think very much of his accomplishments during his previous terms of office. I was informed that during his term of office, he did not do his duties as treasurer. What I did that

angered [Dave Abramson] is that I asked to see his monthly budget reports for the year he was in [office].... He never did furnish me with those documents that are supposed to be public.

So after he got through yelling at me..., I gave a speech on what my plans were if I was elected, since my fliers were never posted. While I was giving my speech, Braxton who was recording the debate, kept looking at me and smirking and whispering to Dave and smirking at me some more. Now this behavior down right pissed me off. During the debate there was only one microphone available on stage, so the candidates could ask each other questions and would step down while the other had a chance to answer. It seemed like everytime [sic] I would go up on stage to answer a question, Braxton was trying to cut me off by giving me hand signals like I didn't have anymore [sic] time to answer.

After the debate, I was called into Braxton's office to see if I had performed [an] illegal act [in] my campaign by consulting a former member. I told him that if that was a violation, this whole campaign [was] a joke. I also asked him if he could furnish the documents I requested from Dave, and he looked at me as if I was stupid. He told me that no such documents exist and told me to go review the responsibilities of what a treasurer does because he assured me that they don't report monthly budgets and spending reports. He said they did produce a yearly budget report and that he would give me one. I felt I was being made a fool until I got a hold of the responsibilities of the treasurer. The very first line on the list of responsibilities stated that the treasurer is to make a report each month of the budget and spending. I was extremely mad in that I was constantly given the run around by Braxton and he never gave me a copy of the yearly budget either, and [he] didn't post my fliers at the campuses until two days before the election.

Mark had enclosed a self-addressed stamped envelope for the return of his paper. When I sent it back to him, I included a note stating that his allegations were very serious, and that he might consider bringing them to the attention of President Moore and to the *Coyote Press*, the college newspaper.

X

Messages on My Answering Machine

On May 19, I departed for the East Coast. I left Mike Green and Venus, the department secretary, the telephone numbers at which they could reach me, and then I relaxed. It was wonderful to be away from all the controversy surrounding the European trip and the travel stipend proposal. I was confident that Mike could handle any problems that might arise. As for the travel stipend proposal, I had done all I could; its fate now rested in the hands of the Student Government and the students who were lobbying for it.

I visited my father and stepmother in New York for a few days, before continuing on to Washington on Sunday, May 23. The week that followed was fascinating. Congresswoman Shelley Berkley graciously allowed me to follow her virtually everywhere she went, from morning to night, for the entire week. I attended the convention of the America-Israel Public Affairs Committee and the banquet of the Service Employees International Union. I sat in on numerous meetings with lobbyists. I listened to Shelley make a speech in a House committee, and hold a teleconference on Medicare with constituents back in Nevada. I watched her cast countless votes on the floor of the House. I even went to a veterans rally, and to a meeting of the House Democratic Caucus attended by Vice President Gore. In short, I got a taste of what it's like to be a freshman member of the House of Representatives.

I found the meetings with lobbyists particularly interesting. At one luncheon, the conversation turned to the issue of term limits. "If they enact term limits," observed one lobbyist, "then members of Congress will all be inexperienced, and their staffs will have all the power. I guess they could put term limits on staff too. Then we lobbyists would have all the power." He smiled wryly. "Come to think of it, term limits are not such a bad idea."

On another occasion, during a breakfast meeting, an affable lobbyist struck up a conversation with me. He was a senior partner of a prominent Washington law firm. I told him about the upcoming trip to Europe that Senator Reid had helped me to organize.

"You know," said the lobbyist, "you might consider naming the program after Senator Reid."

I nodded. "His office certainly gave me lots of help."

He shook my hand, and smiled warmly. "If there's anything that I can ever do for you, make sure to give me a call." He handed me his business card.

I took the card, and handed him one of mine. "Actually, there might be something that you could help me with," I told him.

He nodded. "Sure. Go for it."

"It has to do with that trip to Europe. This year there were several bright students who wanted to go, but couldn't afford it. Any chance you might be able to donate some money to CCSN to provide scholarships for next year's trip?"

"Possibly," he replied. "It sounds like a great program. How much does it cost per student?"

"About $3,000."

"That's all? Quite a bargain! I don't think that should be much of a problem for us. Make sure to get in touch with me after you get back to Vegas. Oh, and don't forget my suggestion about naming the program after Harry Reid."

That was just about the only occasion during that very hectic week that thoughts of my job back in Las Vegas crossed my mind. But on Thursday night, May 27, Shelley caught a plane back to Las Vegas for the Memorial Day weekend, and my visit to the nation's capital began to wind down. On Friday morning I conducted a series of interviews with Shelley's staff. In the afternoon, I assumed the role of tourist, and visited the Supreme Court.

It was on Friday that I finally thought about checking my messages back home. I dialed in to my answering machine, and heard the following message that Gertrude had left a week earlier, on May 21: "I had a disastrous meeting with Silverman, and he threw me off campus. I should never have gone in alone. I was warned. He's a monster!"

I called Gertrude back right away. "Lee," she said. "I marched right into Silverman's office and demanded that he give me an explanation. Chris Chairsell, the provost of the Charleston campus, was there. At first Silverman refused to speak to me. But when I wouldn't go away, he started waving around a piece of paper, claiming that someone had lodged a complaint against me. I asked him who it was, and he refused to say. I tried to grab the piece of paper out of his hand, and he started screaming, claiming that I'd tried to assault him. Imagine that, a sixty-eight-year-old lady like me, assaulting a 350 pound man! If I hadn't been on the verge of tears at that point, I probably would have laughed. He said that Chairsell was going to escort me off campus, and that if I refused to go, he would call campus security. He said that I was not allowed to come back onto campus ever again. I said to him, 'You should be ashamed of yourself! You're a monster!'"

Gertrude started to cry. "I was just so upset at that point. I should have let him call the police. The newspapers would have loved it: 'Police Throw Grandmother Off Campus.' But I was just too upset. I let Chairsell escort me to my car, and then I drove home."

I comforted Gertrude as best I could. Before I hung up, I suggested the possibility that her firing might be in retaliation for her argument with Larry Braxton over the travel stipends. I suggested that she get a lawyer. Gertrude vowed that, not only was she going to get a lawyer, but that she was going to call up the newspapers as well.

I spent the weekend sightseeing in Washington, and then flew to Florida on Monday, May 31, to visit my mother and stepfather for a few days.

On June 2, I got a call from Venus, the PRS department secretary. "Lee," she said, "Page just told me that he cancelled your European politics class for the summer session."

I felt like someone had poured a bucket of ice water on me. "What? Why did he do that? The students going on the trip won't be able to get credit!"

"I don't know," said Venus. "He told me that the order came down from Silverman himself."

"From Silverman? The last time I spoke with him, he said that the class was going forward, and he sent Charles and me down to see Page to make sure that class got into the schedule."

"I don't know why he did it, Lee. I've never heard of something like this before. I don't even have a way to contact the students to let them know that the class is cancelled. When they deleted the course from the computer, they deleted the names of the students who had enrolled in it."

"I can't believe this!" I cried. "Is Charles there?"

Venus said that he was out, and I left an urgent message for him to call me. I then asked to speak to Mike Green. For once, Mike was as surprised as I was, and he could shed no light on the situation.

I hung up, and checked my office voice mail. There were several messages from students who had signed up for the trip. They each said that the computer was not allowing them to enroll in the European politics class, and when they called the Admissions Office to find out why, they were told that the class had been cancelled.

"I can't believe this is happening," I told my mother, my voice choked with emotion.

I picked up the phone and called Cal Chadwick. "Cal," I asked urgently, "what happened at the Student Government meeting?"

"Nothing, really. Niecey passed the gavel to Dave Abramson, and announced that all outstanding business from the previous senate had expired. I asked Dave if he would re-introduce the scholarships at the next Student Government meeting, like he'd promised. He said that he wanted to wait for you to get back, and then discuss the matter. I'm pretty bummed out."

I told Cal that Silverman had cancelled the European politics course.

"Oh," mumbled Cal. "Now I understand what Silverman meant!"

"What are you talking about?"

135

"While I was on my way to the Student Government meeting, I saw Silverman talking with a black man just down the hall from the meeting room. It was out in front of the provost's office."

"Black man? It wasn't Braxton?"

"No, an older guy."

"It must have been Thomas Brown," I said. Brown served as provost at the Cheyenne campus as well as vice president for human resources. His office was next door to the room where the Student Government held their meetings. "What did Silverman say to him?"

"I only caught one sentence, since I was just walking past. But Silverman said, 'Hopefully he won't turn out like Lee Miller.'"

"They must have been planning to cancel my class on the very day that I left town!" I exclaimed. "They were just waiting for me to get out of the way so that I couldn't protest! This is outrageous!" I was furious. However dirty the politics in Washington were, I decided, they couldn't hold a candle to those of CCSN.

I tried calling Charles again at his office, and left an urgent message on his voice mail. I also tried him at home, and left a message with his wife.

I did not get much sleep that night. I tossed and turned, angry with Silverman for canceling the class, unable to fathom why he would do this to my students.

The next morning I tried calling Charles again at home and at his office, but was unable to reach him. I left another message with his wife and another on his office voice mail.

I called Venus as soon as the PRS department office opened. "Some of your students called the office to find out why your European class was cancelled," she said. "I told them that I didn't know, but I took down their names and numbers and told them that I'd have you call them as soon as you get back into town."

"Thanks," I said. "This whole thing makes no sense. Do you have any idea what's going on?"

"I just don't know, Lee. Page said that the order came down from Silverman, but he wouldn't tell me why."

"This is crazy, Venus. Charles still hasn't called me back. The students aren't going to get credit. I've put tons of work into this class, and now I'm not even going to get paid."

"Why don't you sign up to teach a distance ed American government class over the summer, Lee? You just taught one in the spring, so it won't take much preparation. I'll do whatever I can to help you set it up."

I tried without success to sound enthusiastic about her suggestion. "Thanks. I'll call Ruth and check into that possibility."

I wasn't sure it was even worth the trouble. I had done all the work for the European class, and now I could not teach it. Most of the students who had signed up for the European trip had already taken the American government class with me. They could not get credit for repeating the class. What bothered me most was not the lost income, but the terrible injustice done to my students.

Despite this, I took Venus' advice and called Ruth Strode at the Distance Education office. She told me that there was just barely enough time to set up a course for me, but that she and Venus would take care of it.

"I'll call Charles right after I get off the phone with you," promised Ruth. "I'll need to get his approval by the end of the day on Friday for the course to go forward."

Next I called up Candace Kant, the incoming chair of the Faculty Senate, and Linda Foreman, the NFA president. They both sounded shocked by what had happened, and neither could shed any light on the situation.

I flew home to Las Vegas, arriving the following evening, Friday, June 4. On my answering machine I found several messages from students inquiring about why the class was cancelled. There was also a message from Ruth Strode, saying that Charles had not returned her call, and therefore the distance ed class was not a possibility. There was one additional message:

Dr. Miller, my name is Thomas Brown. I'm associate vice president for human resources. I'm calling for Dr. Silverman. Dr. Silverman would like to meet with you regarding your contract on Monday, June 7. Uh…. He asked me to notify you that the System's legal counsel will be present at this meeting and that you may, if you so desire, bring a representative or an attorney with you. The meeting will be held on the West Charleston campus, Building C, Room 250B, at 8:00 a.m. in the morning. That's Dr. Silverman's office.

"Oh, shit!" I cried. "Silverman's going to fire me!" Then I remembered the conversation that Cal had overheard between Brown and Silverman on the day that I left town. "They've been planning this since the day I left for Washington! They waited until I was in Congress with Shelley Berkley before they fired me!" I felt like my world was disintegrating.

I tried calling Charles. This time Mrs. Okeke did not answer the phone. It was Charles himself.

"Charles," I gasped, practically in tears, "what's going on?"

"Lee," he replied in a sing-song voice, as if he was reciting some lines, "I've been instructed to tell you that there will be a meeting with Dr. Silverman on Monday. I advise you to attend. And I have nothing else to say." Then he hung up on me.

Next, I called up Linda Foreman. "Lee, I'm so sorry," she said. "I had no idea that it would come to this. You know, after I spoke to you yesterday, I called up Page to find out why your class was cancelled. He wouldn't give me any information at all, which is very strange for him. But he did say that he thought you were getting a bum rap." Linda said she would check into whether NFA would pay for an attorney to represent me.

I called up Mike Green. He was so shocked that, for the first time since I had met him, he was at a loss for words. "You should call Al Balboni," he suggested at last. "If anyone knows what's going on, it's Balboni."

I took Mike's advice. "Hi, Al, this is Lee M—" I began.

Al cut me off in a voice as cold as ice. "I will have nothing to do with you. Please do not call me again, or I will regard it as harassment." Then he hung up on me.

I was so shocked that I dropped the phone. I sat there staring at it for several minutes until it began to beep with the tone indicating that it was off the hook. My hands were shaking so much that I almost dropped it again when I tried to hang it up.

It took me quite a while to regain enough composure to make another call. I took some deep breaths and called Candace. "I can't believe that they're doing this to you, Lee!" exclaimed the chair of the Faculty Senate. "No one told me anything about this. You should get Richard Segerblom to represent you. He goes by the nickname 'Tick.' He's the best employment attorney in town, and he has great connections. His mother has been in the state legislature for as long as I can remember. You should also insist that Silverman delay his meeting with you, so that you can consult with your attorney in advance."

"Thanks. I'll get a hold of Mr. Segerblom," I mumbled in response. I started to tremble. "Candace, can they really fire me over this? I didn't do anything wrong!"

"I have no idea what this is about. But the good news is that the UCCSN Code states that if they decide not to renew your contract, they have to let you know by March 30. And they also have to inform you of the reasons. So they have to offer you a contract for the next year, although they may offer you a lump sum. You should make sure to meet with Linda Foreman and Frazine Jasper over the weekend. Frazine handles legal defense issues for NFA. Ask Frazine if NFA will pay for Tick to represent you. But the most important thing is this: don't go into that meeting without an attorney."

"Thanks a lot Candace," I said. "I'm just about out of my mind."

"I know," she said. "Hang in there. And keep me posted."

I did not sleep much that night. The next day I called Mike Green. He told me that Al had refused to talk with him about me. Linda Foreman also told me that Al had refused to talk. But she gave me the good news that NFA would pay for up to five hours with Tick Segerblom.

Mike called me again a little later. "Lee, if Silverman wants to meet with you first thing Monday morning, you'd better talk to Tick right away. I called up Gene Segerblom and got Tick's home phone number." Mike seemed to know just about every important politician in southern Nevada, including Assemblywoman Gene Segerblom, Tick's mother.

I called up Tick, and his wife told me that he was out of town and would not be back until the following evening, Sunday.

I was a wreck all weekend. I hardly slept, and walked around in a daze. I felt as if my life was crumbling around me. My boss was firing me for no reason I could figure out, and several of my friends and colleagues refused to speak to me. All that I'd worked so hard to build over the past year was coming apart.

On Sunday, Nathan Taylor returned my call. "They can't do this to you, Dr. Miller! All along you've been fighting for the students at

CCSN, and all along bastards like Braxton have been opposing you. This isn't fair! They can't fire you for doing a great job! If you want, I'll ask Senator James to call Richard Moore about this."

"Thanks, Nathan," I said. "I really appreciate your support. But first thing I think I should do is consult with my attorney." I told him that I was trying to get Tick Segerblom. Nathan was impressed.

That evening, I tried calling Tick Segerblom again. This time he was home.

"I'm sorry to bother you at home," I said. "My name is Lee Miller. I'm an instructor at CCSN. Mike Green gave me your number."

"So, what do you want?" asked the lawyer impatiently.

"Bob Silverman is planning to fire me, apparently. He wants me to meet with him first thing tomorrow morning, and suggested that I bring a lawyer." I then, briefly explained what had occurred.

"Okay," said Tick. "Call Silverman. Tell him to call my office to re-schedule that meeting at a time when I can go."

"Sure," I said. "I guess I should meet alone with you to discuss things before we meet with Silverman."

"No point in that," said Tick. "Would be a waste of your money. Nothing for us to discuss until we know what they're accusing you of."

I swallowed. "Can they really fire me over this scholarship thing?"

"They can fire you for 'disloyalty' or any other reason that they can think of," said Tick grimly. "I don't think you have any recourse."

Afterwards, I called Linda and told her about my conversation with Tick.

"Don't be put off by his gruffness," she said. "Tick is the best there is. He'll get you the best deal possible. But, why don't you meet me at my office at 7:45 tomorrow morning. You've got to call Silverman before 8:00. You can call from my office."

"Thanks," I said. "I could use some moral support."

"I'm on your side," said Linda. "Oh, I meant to tell you. I spoke to Page. I told him that I'd thought that this thing about your European trip had been settled recently. He replied that he also had thought it had been settled. He told me that he's not sure what he's at liberty to say, because, he said, 'there's a whole lot of crap coming down.'"

140

"Yeah," I said. "I know exactly where it all landed."

The last person I called that day was Steve Sisolak. "Tick is a great attorney," said the regent. "Tell him that I'm willing to help in any way that I can."

"I appreciate that," I said.

"I mean it. And make sure to give me a call tomorrow to let me know what happens."

At 7:15 a.m. on Monday, June 7, I loaded up my car and headed for the Cheyenne campus of CCSN. It was the first day of class for the summer term. I had everything ready to teach my American politics class and my European politics class. But my mind was not on teaching that day.

I arrived at Linda Foreman's office at 7:35. She was already there. "I can't believe this is happening," I whined, on the verge of tears. "I've put everything I've got into this job. I've been working sixty hours a week. My students love me. I have great evaluations. I've brought in all these guest speakers, developed all these innovative programs, I got awarded grants to build an internship program and to go to Washington. I can't believe they're doing this to me."

"Me neither," said Linda, giving me a big hug. I sat there with her, blabbering on and on about the injustice of it all, and she lent me a sympathetic ear. After a while, she glanced at her watch. "Time to call Bob," she said.

At 7:55 a.m., I called Silverman's office. I got his voice mail. I left a message asking him to call my lawyer, Richard Segerblom, to re-schedule the meeting at a time when Segerblom could be present. I also told Silverman that I would be at Linda's office until I had to go to class at 9:40, and that if he wanted to reach me, he could call me there.

A few minutes later, Linda's phone rang. She answered, and then handed the phone to me. It was JoAnn, Silverman's secretary. "Dr. Silverman is in his office," she said, "meeting with some people. I expect him to call you back soon, so please don't go anywhere."

I waited a few minutes, and Silverman himself called. "I don't want you to go to your 9:40 class," he said. "Someone else will be there to take care of it."

The words cut like a knife. They had already replaced me. "Okay," I said mournfully. "But...," I stammered, "what about my European politics class this afternoon?"

There was silence at the other end of the line for a few seconds. "I'll — I'll take care of it. I don't want you going to any of your classes until you meet with me. Understand?"

"Uh-huh," I muttered.

"Good. I asked JoAnn to call your lawyer to re-schedule the meeting."

"Uh-huh," I muttered despondently.

Silverman hung up.

I recounted the conversation to Linda. "Good," she observed. "They'll think twice before pulling anything, now that Tick is representing you." She scratched her head. "Do you have a copy of your evaluations?"

"All except for spring. They weren't available yet when I left for Washington."

"If you have good evaluations, they can't claim that they're firing you because you're a lousy teacher. If I were you, I'd get a hold of your spring evals right away. Things like that have a tendency to disappear."

I thanked Linda, and headed for the PRS department office. Sure enough, the official student evaluation forms from three of my five classes were missing. Fortunately, I'd drafted my own anonymous unofficial evaluation forms. My forms went into much greater detail than the generic forms required for all classes at CCSN. The college statistical office had scored my unofficial evaluation forms, and had returned the results directly to me via campus mail. I picked up the envelope at my office and examined its contents for the first time. The students had given me glowing reviews.

The meeting with Silverman was re-scheduled for 5:30 that evening. Linda sent Fred Hymes, vice president of NFA for grievances, to represent the faculty association. Fred and I sat across from JoAnn in the anteroom to Silverman's office, waiting for Tick to arrive. I fidgeted in my chair, my heart racing from the anxiety as the minutes ticked by. Tick was late. He finally arrived at 5:50.

I jumped to my feet as he entered the waiting room. "Lee Miller?" he asked. He was a stocky man with blond hair, in his forties, wearing a rumpled navy suit.

"Glad to meet you," I said, shaking his hand.

"I'm Richard Segerblom," he said. "Sorry I'm late. I was coming from downtown. The traffic was awful."

JoAnn buzzed Silverman, and then led us into his office. The room was large, with a heavy wooden desk just ahead, and a conference table off to the right. Sunlight streamed in from the windows beyond the conference table. Memories flooded my mind of the two occasions on which I previously had entered that room. The first time was in the summer of 1997, when Richard Moore had rudely left me there, ordering me to wait for some unknown "Bob." The second time was during the summer of 1998, when Moore had interrupted my job interview with Silverman to ask for advice about which movie to see over the weekend.

In addition to Silverman and Thomas Brown, there were two men wearing business suits whom I'd never seen before. Silverman introduced them as Kwasi Nyamekye and Karl Armstrong, lawyers from the office of the UCCSN general counsel. I had previously spoken to Kwasi over the phone, and it was he who had drafted the memo stating that only the president could ask for a legal opinion about the scholarship proposal. I never before had met Armstrong. But Tick knew them both, and greeted them warmly.

Silverman asked us to be seated. "I want to keep this short," he said. "Dr. Miller, we have decided not to renew your tenure-track status. We are offering you a one-year terminal contract. You will receive full pay and benefits for one year. For that year, you will be assigned at home. You will have no teaching assignment." He paused, and looked at me. "Do you have any questions?"

"What do you mean, I'll be 'assigned at home'?"

"That means," said Silverman in a pleasant voice, "that you can stay at home or get another job or move out of state or do whatever you want for the next academic year. The one thing that you cannot do is teach at CCSN. You will need to clear out your office, return your keys, and complete a clearance certificate by June 30. You are, of course, free to visit the campus like any other member of the public. But you won't be teaching here any longer."

143

I nodded slightly. I was shocked and angry.

Tick, who had been sitting there with his eyes half closed, opened them wide and leaned forward toward Silverman. "Are you alleging that my client committed any illegal acts?"

Silverman glanced at the two UCCSN attorneys, and then back at Tick. "No," he said. "We are alleging no illegal acts."

I glanced at Tick, but he had closed his eyes again, as if he was asleep.

I turned to Silverman. "I'd like to know why you're doing this," I demanded forthrightly.

A short chuckle escaped Silverman's lips. "No, I'm not going to say anything about that here. If you want an answer to that question, you'll have to write me a letter within the next fifteen days requesting an explanation."

I looked at Tick, but he remained silent. I sighed. "Fine," I said to Silverman. "One more thing. What about the European trip, and the class?"

"I've decided to allow the trip to go forward. We would prefer that you do not accompany the students on this trip. As for the class —" Silverman coughed at this point — "the class was cancelled due to low enrollment. I've decided to reinstate it. There will be another instructor teaching it."

I bit my tongue, to keep from lashing out at the man. "He lies so well," I thought. I knew for a fact that the class had *not* been cancelled due to low enrollment. I had an e-mail from Page stating that classes would not be cancelled due to low enrollment until the end of late registration, which was not for another four days.

Silverman now looked at Tick, despite the fact that he was addressing me. "You also have the option to resign, if you wish. You can work out the arrangements with Mr. Armstrong."

Tick nodded.

Silverman rose, followed by his lawyers. Fred, Tick, and I followed their lead. Tick shook hands with the other attorneys. Then he shook Silverman's hand, and headed for the door. Fred was already walking in that direction. Only Silverman and I remained. Silverman now stood facing me. He hesitated for a moment, and then shook my hand. At that point, I felt more inclined to break the man's arm than to shake his hand. I stared silently into Silverman's eyes as he gave my hand a quick shake. Then he backed away. I continued to stare at him for a moment, and then I walked out the door. I heard it close behind me. I followed Tick and Fred through the waiting room and out into the hallway. My hands were not trembling at all.

"In twenty-two years," said Fred, shaking his head, "I've never seen anything like this."

Tick nodded. "They normally don't do this except in a case of rape or theft."

My eyes opened wide. "Do you think that they're accusing me of...?"

"No," said Tick. "Silverman said that they aren't alleging any illegal acts. I'll get in touch with Armstrong and see if I can find out anything else."

We walked out to the parking lot. The heat was stifling. Pools of water momentarily shimmered on the black asphalt, and then the mirages disappeared as we approached them. The three of us shook hands, and then we got into our separate cars and drove away.

I spent the evening on the phone talking to my girlfriend, Beth (who had taken a job in Los Angeles), my mother, Mike Green, Linda Foreman, and Candace Kant, among other people. Nothing seemed real. I felt like I was in a dream. No, it was more like a nightmare. I probably would have been hysterical, had I not been so worn out from stress and lack of sleep. I just did not seem to have the energy for hysteria. Everyone I spoke to expressed words of shock and words of sympathy. Candace also gave me a piece of advice. She suggested that I hold off from writing to Silverman to ask for an explanation until I had discussed the matter with Tick. If Silverman put his grievances against me in writing, she said, it would thereafter exist as a permanent record in my personnel file, thereby making it harder for me to get another job.

The next day I called Sally, a student who had been enrolled in both of my summer classes, and who was planning to go on the trip. "An adjunct instructor took over your American government class," Sally told me. "He was pretty unorganized, and very boring. I'm not at all impressed." Sally's new instructor was John, the same adjunct instructor who had failed to show up at my unemployment insurance hearing in August 1998. He was also the instructor whom Charles had considered firing just a few months earlier, due to students' complaints about his poor teaching. Charles had sent me to evaluate him. I had felt bad for the guy; I gave John a bunch of suggestions and recommended to Charles that he give him another chance. How ironic that John now had replaced me.

"You know," continued Sally, "I had to call up Silverman and chew him out on the phone so that he would reinstate the European class. At first he refused to budge. Then I told him that I had paid several thousand dollars to go on the European trip, expecting to receive academic credit, and if he didn't reinstate it, I was going to sue."

"Good for you," I said.

"Anyway, Sam Sarri, the instructor they sent to teach the European course, seems to be good. I would have preferred it if you had been the instructor, but I think that Dr. Sarri will work out just fine."

"He normally teaches economics," I said. "I'm surprised they asked him to teach a political science course. But he seems like a nice guy. I'm glad things are working out for you."

I also called Bettyann at EF Tours to let her know that I had been fired and that the scholarships had been cancelled. I asked whether it would be possible to send someone else to lead the European trip in my place. She told me that the group leader cannot be changed, and that if Silverman decided now to send Sam or any other instructor on the trip, that person would be treated as a late applicant and probably would have to go on a separate flight from the students. Bettyann re-priced the trip, based on twelve paying participants, rather than twenty, and told me that each person would have to pay an additional $390. My heart sank. This was so unfair. I felt like I had let the students down.

On Wednesday, June 9, Tick called me. "Good news," he said. "Spoke to Armstrong. They have no accusations of wrongdoing. Armstrong said that you had just 'pissed off Silverman and Moore,' and therefore they decided to get rid of you."

"That's good news," I said, my spirits rising a bit for the first time in a week. I was very relieved that they had not decided to fire me on some trumped-up charges. "What should I do now?"

"You have a couple of options," said Tick. "You can resign, but then they won't pay you."

"That's not a very good option," I said.

"You can also let them fire you. If you want, you can sue them later. You're guaranteed a full year of pay, and you have two years to decide whether or not you want to sue them."

"What about writing to Silverman and asking for an explanation?"

"If you want to keep open the option of a lawsuit, that would be a good idea. Given that they have nothing on you, they aren't going to be able to come up with a very strong explanation. That will weaken their case. After they give you an explanation, you can appeal the decision. If you want to keep open the option of suing, you should make sure to jump through all their hoops, that is, to exhaust all your other remedies."

"That makes sense," I said. "I wonder, is there any chance that I'll be able to get the money that CCSN owes me? I'm supposed to get a $1,500 grant for the trip to Washington that I just returned from. I also was supposed to get paid about $10,000 for teaching my two classes this summer."

"I'm not very optimistic," said Tick. "But I'll check with Armstrong."

Later that day I spoke to Gertrude. She had regained her spunk, and was busy collecting stories about other people who had been wronged by Silverman. "Lee, remember the time that I introduced you to that evil man, Bill Cassell, in the International Student Center? He started chewing you out over your European trip. Well, I never told you this, but after you left, he bad-mouthed you around the office quite a bit."

"I didn't think that you'd noticed how rude he was to me!"

"How could I *not* notice!" exclaimed Gertrude.

"But you never commented on it to me after we left Cassell's office."

"Don't you think that I was embarrassed? I felt really bad about the way he treated you. That's why I dragged you off so quickly to meet with some of my friends among the faculty. I wanted the both of us to forget about it as soon as possible."

"Maybe Cassell had something to do with my firing, and yours," I mused. "Both of us got fired for no apparent reason around the same time. Cassell is really close to Richard Moore, I understand."

147

"He's a horrible man. Everyone hates him. He treated me like dirt!" spat Gertrude.

"Isn't it strange that the same group of people are mad at you and at me. Let's see, there's Cassell, Braxton, and —"

"And that bastard Silverman!"

"Strange."

I was feeling pretty depressed about losing my job. I felt that no one appreciated the hard work I had done on behalf of my students. It was at this moment of despair that I got an e-mail from George Turner, one of my best students, inviting me to his retirement party. George was a great writer, articulate in class discussions, and had a keen interest in politics. He was retiring after several decades in the Air Force. I wrote back thanking him for the invitation, and let him know about my dismissal. George was well aware of the travel stipend controversy. This is what he wrote back:

Sorry to hear about the upper crust attempting to do away with such an outstanding educator. If there is anything I can do, let me know. Always follow your heart and do what your gut tells you is right. It usually is. I'd like to tell you a little story that might give you a little insight as to how I stay so positive.

A while back (about 22 years ago) a gentleman confronted me at a graduation dinner for the USAF in Europe Noncommissioned Officer Academy. I had been to the NCO Academy in Germany as a young, new to the service airman, telling senior NCOs what we troops expected in a supervisor. I didn't know this gentleman from Adam. He said, "I understand you are very opinionated."

I said yes I was — when I believed in something strong enough to speak out.

He then said, "Good, we need people like you to tell us old farts what we need to hear and not what we want to hear. Everything is not always so rosy."

I didn't understand what he was talking about. Then he said, "Keep that up. You are going to piss off people along your career path, but it's people like you that are going to keep us all straight and make this a better Air Force."

That gentleman was the senior enlisted advisor to the Commander-in-Chief for U.S. Air Forces in Europe. He later became the Chief Master Sergeant of the Air Force, the highest enlisted person in the Air Force. I met him again about five years later in Hawaii, while I was attending the NCO Leadership School, and he remembered me for that small incident and short meeting while in Germany.

I have lived by that conversation my whole career. Yes, I have pissed people off, been passed over for promotion and now I'm retiring from the Air Force.

Several months ago, former Chairman of the Joint Chiefs, Gen. Colin Powell, gave a speech to a bunch of civilians, and said, "Integrity is doing the right thing all the time regardless of who is watching, if anyone. Doing the right thing is going to piss people off, but that's what happens when you make decisions that force others to re-evaluate their substandard performance."

So, the moral of this is to do what you know is right regardless of who is offended because you have to live with yourself and integrity is more important than what others feel or think.

Maybe I'm missing the mark here, but the tone of your e-mail gave me the impression that the leadership of the school was attempting to eliminate an educator because that educator was doing the right thing when they were attempting to just maintain the status quo. That never leads to improvement and improvement is what we all should be striving for with all that we do.

Good luck and stay positive. You have a loyal former student here that thinks you are a credit to the teaching profession. As a leader in the community, you are instructing students not only about what is in the lesson books, but also teaching about life. Stay in touch.

George Turner

XI

Europe

Several months earlier I had made plans to spend a long weekend in Los Angeles. My girlfriend Beth had taken a new job in LA back in April, and I had been planning to visit her on June 10–14.

I also had a screen test to look forward to. On a whim, just before I left for Washington, I had answered an ad in the *Chronicle of Higher Education*. A producer was looking for a college professor for his new adventure/historical show for cable TV. The show was to be called "Eco-Explorers," and was to feature a group of outdoor enthusiasts following in the footsteps of the great explorers of past centuries. The producer had left me a message while I was in Washington, and had asked me to come to LA for a screen test on the weekend during which I was planning to visit Beth.

It was a great relief to get out of Las Vegas, and for a time to leave behind my anxieties about my job at CCSN and the trip to Europe. It was great to see Beth, and the prospect of becoming a TV star was exciting. I began to fantasize about becoming famous, and rubbing it in the nose of Bob Silverman and his allies.

The screen test was lots of fun. We drove up into the San Gabriel Mountains north of Los Angeles. The crew filmed a group of prospective cast members — including myself — rock climbing and mountain biking. I also had to recite some ridiculous lines on camera: "It was on this very spot in the year 1492 that Pocahontas was executed for beheading her fifth husband Coronado for having an extramarital affair." It was very hard to keep a straight face while mangling history so badly.

I was one of only two college professors whom the producer had invited to take the screen test. The other half-dozen people were professional actors. In the end, the producer chose three of the actors. In retrospect, I decided that either my cleavage had been too small or that my personality had not been outrageous enough for the job. The producer offered the job to the following candidates: (1) the most attractive actress, (2) a man who had insisted on taking his dog on the screen test, and who cracked jokes non-stop while chain-smoking cigarettes (which was particularly ironic for a show called "Eco Explorers"), and (3) a lesbian with a crew-cut who had muscles much bigger than mine. The third struck up a conversation with Beth at one point. But the actress quickly lost interest once Beth let her know that she was my girlfriend. Her parting words to Beth were, "as long as he fucks you good, you should be okay with him."

I dreaded returning to Las Vegas, but return I did on Monday, June 14. After further consultations with Tick, I drafted the following letter to Silverman:

Dear Dr. Silverman:

I am invoking my right under Section 5.2.3 of the Personnel Policy for Faculty to request a statement in writing of the reasons that I have been denied reappointment. As stated in the Personnel Policy, I must receive your response within 15 calendar days (June 30, 1999).

Sincerely,

Lee R. Miller

I waited a couple of weeks for a reply. Meanwhile, I still had to deal with the issue of the trip fee increase. When Braxton finally had succeeded in killing the travel stipends, he had done more than prevent six needy students from taking part in the trip. Without those six participants, the average price per applicant went up by nearly $400. I seethed with the injustice of this, and the students were furious when I told them that they each would have to pay an additional $390.

I considered two options. I could let the students eat the loss, which I felt was very unfair. Or I could ignore the fact that I had just lost my job and pay the difference out of my own pocket. I agonized over this decision for several days. Finally, on June 16, I decided on a third option: I would pay for Beth's ticket. I had promised to take my girlfriend on this trip, utilizing one of the free tickets. I checked with EF and they told me that if I sent them $2,999 — the value of Beth's free ticket — it would reduce the extra cost per person from $390 to only $167. This is exactly what I did and the students were very grateful.

In the end, I put in over six hundred hours organizing this trip (not counting the actual time spent in Europe), I spent over $3,000 of my own money, and I lost my job as a result. I also lost about $10,000 worth of summer pay. But I felt good about my decision to pay for Beth's ticket. When the world around you seems rife with injustice, there is no greater pleasure than knowing that you have done the right thing.

Sally, a student in my — I mean Sam Sarri's — European politics class, had asked me repeatedly to get in touch with Sam so that he could coordinate his curriculum with my trip. Sally had told me that she was making this request on behalf of all the students in the class.

I felt kind of uneasy about this, given the circumstances under which Sam had taken over the class. But Sally told me that this was important for her education, so I could not in good conscience refuse her request.

On June 15, I sent Sam a copy of the itinerary for the trip, as well as my syllabus. We exchanged a series of e-mails over the next couple of days, in which he described what he planned to do in the class, and I offered to share with him the notes that I had prepared. He politely declined my offer. I called Sally to let her know.

"You know, Dr. Sarri told us that we shouldn't bother with the reader that you prepared for us," she mentioned.

"What? He told you not to read those articles?" I was shocked. I had spent weeks selecting a series of articles, mostly from the *Economist* magazine, on the topics that we were scheduled to discuss with officials from the European Union and NATO.

I sent Sam an e-mail, telling him that I had selected the articles in the reader specifically to prepare the students for the meetings we had scheduled, and asking him not to dissuade the students from reading them. Sam replied as follows:

Dear Dr. Miller:

I, indeed, worked as an econometrician, political economist, and professional technical translator/interpreter (French, English, Classical Arabic), along with the EEC [European Economic Community, the predecessor of the European Union], the French Ministry of Finance, and the Maghrebin (Morocco, Tunisia, Algeria) governments, during periodic times from 1976 through 1982. My master's thesis, with the University of Lille (1979), France focused on Tatcherism [sic], fiscality [sic] and the EEC enlargement. My Bachelor's memoire, moreover, stressed the Sugar Consumption Keynesian Function and the Politico-economic interpenetrations with North-Africa and the EEC. A good portion of my doctorate with the University of Paris polarized [sic] around the economics and politics of the european monetary system (EMS), etc. Henceforth, I humbly feel that my expertise in the european [sic] politics and economics arenas equip me, effectively and considerably, to proceed with PS295, as an honor students class. I, indeed, appreciate your suggestions: "Reader's" journalistic clips and the 1992 textbook. However, as the Instructor of Records [sic], I prefer to proceed with an updated statistical and substantive methodology to comptemporrary [sic] european [sic] parliamentarism, euronomics, and euroculture. My students, furthermore, are very pleased with our collectively selected materials and the updated research political projects. Most of the data, of course, are to be generated from voluminous european websites, especially those of the US DOS, EU, NATO, SHAPE, EC, EEC, UN, EFTA, OECD, GATT, ICJ, and so forth. And whenever they have a sound opportunity to meet with a decision-maker (like Professor Didier Mauss of l'Administration Publique Internationale et Francaise) as in Paris, France this July [this was one of the meetings I had arranged], they should be efficaciously equipped to ask the right politocological and economic questions, seeking, thus, plausible empirical responses. Again, I'd appreciate it if you cease phoning or e-mailing.

Best wishes,
Dr. Sarri

I was surprised by Sam's response. All I had asked him to do was to stop dissuading the students from reading the articles I had selected to prepare them for the upcoming meetings. I had not even contacted him of my own volition, but instead at the urging of Sam's students. Not only did he ignore my polite request, but he sent me a summary of his resume, and cc'd Charles, Page, and Silverman.

I felt insulted and humiliated, and considered issuing a response that was equally insulting. Instead I took a deep breath and replied with the utmost respect and humility:

Dear Dr. Sarri,

I am well aware of your impeccable academic credentials, and I wish in no way to give you the impression that I hold you in anything other than high esteem. I have no interest in telling you how to teach PSC 295 or any other class. I have contacted you only because your students requested me to do so.

As you know, your student, [Sally (not her real name)] has contacted me on several occasions, urging me to get in touch with you. She and other students in your course have been concerned that your curriculum, while otherwise excellent, has not covered closely enough the topics to be discussed during our upcoming meetings with public officials.

Unless I recall our communications incorrectly, I have addressed exactly three topics: (1) I urged you to familiarize yourself with the itinerary of the trip so that your students would feel that you are preparing them adequately for the trip, (2) I offered to share with you all of the instructional materials which I had prepared for teaching PSC 295, and (3) I requested that you refrain from discouraging your students from reading the collection of articles that I have made available for them in the bookstore. (These articles are background reading for the meetings we have scheduled.)

I have no other information to convey or requests to make of you.

I am cc'ing [Sally], so that she knows that you would prefer to cease communication with me on these matters. Henceforth, she and the other students will have to deal directly with you on whatever concerns they may have.

I wish you all the best.

Sincerely,

Lee R. Miller

On June 28, Sally and one of the other students planning to go on the trip to Europe told me that they had demanded that Silverman meet with them to discuss their grievances. They planned to demand that CCSN pay for the price increase that resulted when the cancellation of the scholarships reduced the number of persons going on the trip. I wished them the best of luck.

It was that day that I finally cleared out my office. I knew that the act of clearing out my office would force me to accept the fact I had lost a job that had meant a great deal to me. I had dreaded doing this, and had put it off as long as possible. But I faced a deadline of June 30, and I could not procrastinate much longer.

This was one of the hardest things that I'd ever had to do. With each book I removed from the shelf and placed in a cardboard box, I felt the sting of injustice. I choked back tears as I said goodbye to the other instructors with whom I shared the trailer. Then I drove sullenly home.

The following day, I finally received Dr. Silverman's letter explaining why he had fired me:

Dear Dr. Miller:

Your behavior subsequent to the February 4, 1999 evaluation [the one in which Charles had rated my performance as "commendable"] raised considerable concerns about your willingness to comply with the policies and procedures by which the College is governed. The College issued you a NOTICE OF NON REAPPOINTMENT because of your unprofessional behavior with the professionals of this College and our System.

Sincerely,

Robert M. Silverman, Ph.D.

I called up Mike Green, and read him the letter. "I don't know whether to be relieved or outraged," I said. "I'm relieved that they couldn't come up with any good reason to justify firing me. But what Silverman wrote makes no sense! It's not that I broke any College rules, no, he's just concerned about my 'willingness' to follow them! He cites me for unprofessional behavior. I don't know how much more professional I could have been, taking all this bullshit from him and Braxton and Cassell without once losing my temper!"

"It's par for the course, isn't it?" observed Mike.

"How the hell do idiots like this rise to positions of power?"

"Dr. Peter pointed out the principle that, in a bureaucracy, individuals rise to the level of their incompetence."

I couldn't help but laugh.

"Actually, Lee, I envy you in a funny way. Silverman sent you away with a year's salary and a year to look for a new job. But I'm still stuck with him."

"So, you don't think I should fight this? If I did, I'd probably win. I could call up Harry Reid, Shelley Berkley, Steve Sisolak, Kathy Von Tobel —"

"Why bother?" asked Mike abruptly.

The question took me off guard. "What do you mean?"

"Look, Silverman doesn't wipe his ass before getting permission from Moore. That means that the general wants you out. If you force them to reverse their decision to fire you, they'll spend the next four years trying to make your life a living hell. And then they'll quietly deny you tenure. Is that the future you're looking forward to? You should catch the next plane to California and hang out on the beach with Beth. Why fight it?"

I sat there silently pondering his argument for a long moment. "You're probably right," I said at last, "but the thought of just rolling over and letting them have what they want drives me mad."

"So," said Mike, "give Natalie Patton a call. She'd love this story." Mike was friends with Natalie Patton, the reporter who had exposed the scandal of Bill Cassell jetting around the world recruiting foreign students for CCSN.

"I'd love to," I said, glumly, "but Tick advised me to lay low until I sign that contract. He said that I should avoid doing anything to 'antagonize' them, lest they change their minds about giving me that year's salary. In fact, he said that I should probably keep a low profile until I get a new job and collect my last paycheck from them."

"Sounds like good advice," said Mike. "Besides, this gives you a year to plot how to get even."

I laughed. "Yeah, I suppose you're right."

On June 30, I returned to campus to get the final signatures on the "clearance certificate," proving that I had done such things as turning in my keys and returning my photocopy card. Venus wept when I said goodbye to her.

I walked down to the Human Resources Office and handed the clearance certificate to Dawn. She told me that my direct deposit had been cancelled, and that I would have to pick up my paycheck in person. That day, it turns out, was payday, and so I asked her to give me my paycheck. Dawn looked for it, but was unable to locate it. She could not give me an explanation as to what might have happened to it.

"In that case," I said, "I'm keeping this document." I brought the clearance certificate home, and called up Tick.

"They're playing games with me, and I don't like it," I complained to my lawyer. "I cleared out my office, like Silverman asked me to do, and then went to HR to pick up my paycheck. The girl at the counter told me that they don't have it, and she couldn't explain why."

Tick faxed a letter to Karl W. Armstrong, assistant general counsel for UCCSN, inquiring about my paycheck and some other issues:

Dear Mr. Armstrong:

My client attempted to pick up his last paycheck today and was told that it was unavailable. Can you please locate the check and let me know how Professor Miller can obtain it?

Also, Dr. Miller has not yet received his contract for the 1999–2000 school year. Do you know when he will receive that contract? Additionally, I have previously asked you about payment for summer school classes he was scheduled to teach, and the $1,500 stipend he has been awarded. Is Dr. Miller going to receive those monies?

Finally, it my understanding that officials from the Community College are planning to meet with students who will be participating in the European trip. Please let me know as soon as possible what is discussed and/or resolved at that meeting. At this point my client is planning to participate in the trip, so if that conflicts with the College's position we need to know as soon as possible.

Thank you for your continuing cooperation in this matter.

Sincerely,

Richard Segerblom

Just a couple of hours later, Dawn from Human Resources called me. She apologized for her error, explaining that my direct deposit had not been cancelled after all, and that my paycheck had been deposited into my bank account. I checked, and the money was indeed there.

That same day I also wrote to Silverman, denying his allegations, and appealing his decision to fire me:

Dear Dr. Silverman:

I have examined your letter of June 23, 1999, giving reasons for denial of my reappointment. I am invoking my right under Section 5.2.4 of the Personnel Policy for Faculty to request reconsideration of the denial.

I believe that the allegations in your letter are incorrect:
- I have never violated any of the policies or procedures by which the College is governed;
- I have never dealt with College or System officials in an unprofessional manner.

Since you list no specific examples in your letter, I am unable to provide any documentation to support my belief that your allegations are incorrect.

Please promptly direct my request for reconsideration through regular administrative channels, as per Section 5.2.4.

Please be advised that I will be out of the country, July 10, 1999 through July 24, 1999; you will be unable to reach me during that time period.

Sincerely,

Lee R. Miller, Ph.D.

The next day I spoke to Tick again. "Armstrong called me up," he said. "He told me that there's no problem with you going on the trip, and that you'll get paid for one week."

"What's that supposed to mean?" I asked. "I get paid by the credit hour, not by the week."

"How many weeks was the class?"

"Four," I said.

"Maybe he means that you'll get one-fourth of your pay."

"I put in about six hundred hours preparing for this trip and the class that goes along with it. I should get my full pay!"

"Well, I'm just telling you what he said."

"What else did he say?" I asked.

"He said you'll get your contract the same time everyone else does. End of July."

"Uh-huh," I said, anxious about the prospect of leaving the issue of my next year's income up in the air for another month. There was no way I would be able to get another teaching job at this late date. "What about the grant for my trip to Washington?"

"Armstrong said that you won't get that because it's part of your summer school pay."

"That's ridiculous! I was back from Washington before the summer term even began. And, anyway, this is paid for with a federal grant, not the CCSN budget. CCSN only disburses the funds."

Later that day I spoke to David White. This bright young student had been having his own difficulties with a federal grant. He had been an Americorps volunteer, and had decided to use toward the cost of the European trip the grant he had earned from his service. But the money had gotten held up with some red tape. I contacted Senator Reid's office on David's behalf, and they got it straightened out.

"Thanks a lot for the help with the Americorps grant," he said.

"I'm just glad that you're going to be able to join us," I replied. "By the way, did you go to that meeting with Silverman today?"

David told me that Silverman, Page, Charles, Armstrong, and Sam Sarri were there. "All the students in the class went. We told them that we were really unhappy about this whole situation, about the change of instructors and all, and we told them that we thought CCSN should pay for the fee increase for the trip. Silverman said that it wasn't their responsibility, and he refused to pay."

"I'm not surprised," I said.

On July 10, I departed for Europe with a group of twelve Las Vegans. As was the case with other classes I had taught at the community college, these students ranged in age from teenager to senior citizen. They included, among others, a nurse, a retired scientist from the Department of Energy, and a state senator and his wife.

I am very proud that, despite the great opposition I encountered, I refused to cancel this trip. It was a dazzling success. In addition to visiting some of the most beautiful sights in Europe, we learned first-hand about all sorts of interesting political and economic issues.

In Amsterdam, we cruised the canals and visited the house where young Anne Frank and her family had hid from the Nazis during World War II. We also met with health department officials to learn about Dutch drug policies. In the United States, drug abuse is treated as a criminal matter, and drug addicts are sent to prison — a place where drugs are readily available. They go into prison as addicts, and when they are released, they are still addicts. In the Netherlands, we were told, drug abuse is treated as a public health issue. Rather than sending heroin addicts to prison, for example, the government engages in an aggressive outreach and treatment program. They deliver counseling, clean needles, and methadone to addicts in their homes. They also make a distinction between "hard" drugs like heroin and cocaine, and "soft" drugs like marijuana and hashish. Soft drugs, which are considered to be no more dangerous than alcohol, can be purchased in small amounts at "coffee houses" throughout the city. The Dutch officials were proud to tell us that every year the average age of heroin addicts in the city rises, indicating that few new users are getting hooked on this dangerous drug. We had a very enlightening discussion, and even Senator Shaffer was impressed.

After Amsterdam we traveled to the Hague. There we visited the International Court of Justice (the World Court), the Permanent Court of International Arbitration, and the International Criminal Tribunal for the Former Yugoslavia. At the latter institution, we met with senior officials responsible for the prosecution of war crimes, and we attended part of the trial of Zoran Kupreskic, a Bosnian Croat accused of murdering his Muslim neighbors. In the Hague we also met with a Dutch professor to discuss some of the differences between social welfare policies in the U.S. and the Netherlands.

Next we spent several days in Brussels. In addition to touring the sights of this historic city, including the beautiful medieval guild houses, we visited many of the important international institutions located there. At NATO, we discussed with diplomats and military officials the recently completed war in Kosovo. At the European Commission, the executive body of the European Union, we grilled officials about some recent scandals, which had led to the resignation and replacement of the entire membership of that body. At the European Parliament we discussed the expansion of the powers of this institution under the recently signed Treaty of Amsterdam. At the Council of the European Union, we had an amazingly frank discussion with a high-ranking administrator of that powerful body. My students were amazed when he told them what happens when the tiny country of Luxembourg assumes the Presidency of the EU, a post that rotates between member states every six months. Apparently, officials from the government of Luxembourg visit all the universities in their country and select the brightest students. They give these students a crash course in public administration. Then, during the six months that the government of Luxembourg is responsible for running the EU, these students are responsible for running the country of Luxembourg.

Luxembourg was the next stop on our itinerary. We toured the sights of the capital city, a place of narrow cobblestone streets and a castle right out of Sleeping Beauty. We also visited the European Court of Justice — the Supreme Court of the European Union — where we discussed the evolution of EU law with some very knowledgeable officials. The students got a kick out of being allowed to pose for pictures sitting in the chairs of the justices. (No one but the justices themselves may sit in the chairs of the justices of the U.S. Supreme Court.) That evening, a top court administrator invited us to his home for a barbecue.

We also visited the American Cemetery, containing the graves of thousands of American soldiers killed during World War II. I could not help think of the opening day ceremony at CCSN as I gazed upon the grave of General Patton.

Next, we crossed into Germany. After touring the medieval castle at Heidelberg, we traveled to ultra-modern Frankfurt, the financial capital of the EU. There we discussed the launch of the Euro, the new single European currency, with officials at the European Central Bank (the counterpart of the Federal Reserve Board in the United States).

Our final stop was Paris. We took in the sights of the City of Lights, such as the Eiffel Tower and the Louvre Museum. We also received a VIP tour of the French Parliament. In addition, we discussed U.S.-French relations with officials at the Foreign Ministry, and discussed the French constitution during a private luncheon with a renowned professor at the International Institute for Public Administration.

The trip was a spectacular success. All the heartaches I had endured were worth it. My one great regret was that seven bright and eager students had been unable to go on this fantastic trip because of some bizarre political manipulations on the part of CCSN officials.

When we returned to Las Vegas on July 25, the following letter was waiting for me.

Dear Mr. Miller:

I have received your request for reconsideration of your *notice of non-reappointment*. After a review of the materials you submitted and a thorough discussion with Senior Vice President for Academic Affairs, Dr. Robert Silverman, I have decided to uphold the decision to issue you a *notice of nonreappointment*.

Cordially,

Richard Moore, Ph.D.
President

I called up Mike Green. "Sorry to hear that Moore rejected your appeal," he said. "But I can't say that I'm surprised. There's no way Silverman would have fired you without first consulting with Moore."

"I worked so hard this year, Mike," I whined. "It's all so unfair."

"Let this be a lesson to you. You've been under the impression that this college is in business for educational purposes. It's not. You were fired because you put the students' education first. This thing had nothing to do with education. It was all about egos. So, now, you've learned your lesson. Stop working so hard. Just do the minimum, and keep a low profile. That's what administrators want, after all."

"How depressing," I moaned.

"That's life," said Mike. "Anyway, I wanted to tell you about the department meeting we had while you were out of town. I asked Al why you had been fired. He told us you were fired for 'unprofessional behavior.'"

Mike continued: "'What's that supposed to mean?' I asked him. Al refused to answer.

"Then Billy Monkman proposed a motion requesting an explanation from Silverman for your firing. Al called you 'devious and manipulative,' and told us that he would vote against the motion. Billy had to withdraw the motion."

"Why did he have to withdraw it?" I asked.

"Because it would not have been unanimous. Under the circumstances, there was no way Billy could ask untenured faculty to vote for it unless it would pass unanimously. You provided a textbook example of what happens to an untenured faculty member who goes out on a limb and says something that displeases the administration."

I sighed. "Well, I really appreciate the effort," I said.

"I just wish it had been successful," he replied.

I was touched that Billy had attempted to stand up for me. But at that point I had nothing but contempt for a profession that systematically removed the backbones of grown men and women, such that they have the courage to stand up for what is right only when they do so unanimously. What kind of system makes bullies into leaders, and leaders into frightened mice? But I suppose I had been forewarned.

I thought back to my first visit to the PRS department after getting hired full-time. When I had entered the department office, I had noticed that someone had tacked my letter to the editor about the unemployment insurance issue to the bulletin board. As I was introduced to my colleagues for the first time, each of them, in turn, told me that s/he was surprised that I had written that letter to the editor.

"I never would have had the courage to do that, if it had been me that they were considering for a job here," had remarked Jim Fuller, a history instructor. "At least not until after I got tenure."

The comment had surprised me. "I'm not afraid to point out injustice," I had replied. "I couldn't live with myself if I didn't. If this is the sort of place where they hold things like this against you, then it's not the sort of place where I want to work."

I was warned from the start that you have to check your courage and convictions at the door when you become a tenure-track college professor. That was not the sort of lesson that I wished to teach to my students. I hoped that my colleagues were not teaching it to theirs.

A couple of days later, on July 27, I wrote back to Richard Moore:

Dear Dr. Moore:

It was with great disappointment that I read your letter of July 7 informing me of your decision to uphold the issuance of a notice of nonreappointment.

Unless I misunderstand the UCCSN Code, I have exhausted all appeals and I am left with no option but to sign the one-year terminal contract which has been offered me.

I still look forward to receiving a full explanation of why I was issued this notice of nonreappointment. I also look forward to receiving contracts for overload pay for summer 1999, fall 1999, and spring 2000, to which I should be entitled.

Sincerely,

Lee R. Miller, Ph.D.

The "overload pay" to which I referred was a substantial sum of money. Firstly, all political science instructors received one credit of overload pay ($565) per semester. At CCSN the normal teaching load was fifteen credits per semester, while political science instructors were expected to teach sixteen credits. This was because Political Science 101 was a four-credit class, and political science instructors usually taught four classes, or sixteen credits.

The biggest portion of the overload pay, however, was the nearly $10,000 that I was to have earned for teaching two classes over the summer. Although I also had made substantial preparations for my American government course, I felt that it was *particularly* unjust for them to withhold the pay for the European politics course. I had put in some six hundred hours preparing for this class and the associated trip, I had been the students' instructor night and day during the two weeks that we were in Europe, and I had spent over $3,000 of my own money to make it possible for the students to go on this trip.

Later that day, Tina Petrillose from Human Resources called to let me know that my contract was ready. I picked it up and brought it home. There was no way I was going to sign anything without first having Tick take a look at it. Tina said that I needed to sign and return it by July 29, so that I would be sure to get paid on July 30.

When I got home, I carefully examined the document. Aside from the clause stating, "this is a terminal contract which will expire 06/30/2000," it was a standard contract, identical to the one I had signed a year earlier. This, in fact, was a big problem.

"They're trying to screw me again!" I told Tick, after faxing him a copy of the contract. This contract, just like the previous one, listed me at Step 4 (three years of experience). Since instructors' salaries are based on their experience, this meant that I would not receive the salary increase of approximately $1,000 that comes with advancement to Step 5.

Tick called Armstrong. A short while later Tina called me back and said that they had raised me to Step 5. Thank God for lawyers!

XII

The Luckiest Man in the World

That afternoon I went for a rolfing session. Rolfing is a sort of deep tissue massage focused on correcting your posture and the alignment of your body with the force of gravity. I really needed a session after all the traveling, not to mention all the bullshit that had awaited me upon my return. A month earlier, the last time I had seen Steve, the rolfer, I had told him about being fired from my job at CCSN.

Now, Steve had a story to tell me. "It's a really strange coincidence," he said. "I spoke to a former girlfriend, last week. She works in the International Student Center at CCSN. I mentioned that I had a client, Lee Miller, who used to work at CCSN, but who was just fired. 'They got rid of him because they were jealous,' she blurted out. She wouldn't say anything else about it after that. I guess she thought she'd said too much already."

"That's really weird," I said. "The International Student Center is on the Charleston campus. I teach at the Cheyenne campus. I hardly ever go over there, and I don't have anything to do with the International Student Center. I wonder how she knows about my firing."

"Maybe a big topic of gossip."

"That would surprise me. I haven't told very many people at Cheyenne. I hardly know anyone at all at the Charleston campus. I wonder why someone I've never met — someone who works at a different campus — would take an interest in this."

Then it hit me. A certain Bill Cassell ran the International Student Center, and he had been very much opposed to my European trip from the beginning. Gertrude had worked there, and she had been fired. My firing might not have been a topic of interest throughout the whole college, but apparently it was one at the International Student Center. Bill Cassell had it in for both Gertrude and for me, it appeared.

At my urging, Linda Foreman wrote to Silverman, insisting that he release the $1,500 grant for my trip to Washington. Silverman relented, and on August 10, I got a call from Sandra Jackson-Oliver that the contract for the payment of the grant was ready for me to sign.

Sandra, in addition to working at CCSN in the department that handles grants such as this, was a student at CCSN. She had been one of the students who had applied for a travel stipend from the Student Government.

I signed the contract, and handed it back to Sandra.

"You know," she told me, "I called up Niecey after she vetoed the scholarships, and urged her to reverse her decision. She told me that she'd vetoed the money because she felt pressured by all those public officials who supported the project. She said all sorts of crazy things."

I nodded.

"After Dave Abramson was elected president," continued Sandra, "I called him up to ask him to honor his campaign promise to push through the scholarships. He flatly refused. He told me that there were too many 'political problems' associated with it."

"A man of his word," I muttered sarcastically.

As I drove home, I pondered the role that Dave Abramson had played in this affair. It seemed to me that he had played me off against Braxton and Silverman. Dave had told me repeatedly that he supported the travel stipends proposal. He had told my students the same thing, and had made a campaign speech in front of my class promising to do whatever it would take to get the funding passed by the Student Government. It was Dave who had urged me to advertise the stipends, and to set up a committee of faculty to review the applications. It was also Dave who had amended the motion under consideration by the student senate, making the funding contingent upon me contacting the general counsel and the chair of the Board of Regents for their approval. I had taken Dave at his word that he was trying to help, and I had done all the things that he had asked me to do. Every one of them had come back to haunt me later on.

What disturbed me the most about Dave was not what he had said to me, but what others had said that he had told them. There was Al Balboni, who claimed that Dave had been spreading the word that Al had endorsed the stipend proposal, after I had told Dave that Al would take no position on it. Then there was Bob Silverman, who claimed that Dave had told him that he opposed the stipend scheme. Finally, there were Cal Chadwick and Tanya Washington, two of my students who had applied for the stipends. They told me that Dave had promised them privately that the Student Government would pay for them to go on a trip to Europe over the summer — just as long as it was not the trip that I had organized. (To their credit, both students refused his offer.) As soon as he had assumed the presidency, Dave had broken his campaign pledge to push through the stipends. He clearly was not a man of his word.

Not long after that, I was on the radio. KNPR, the local public radio station, had a program called "Making Nevada Home." Every Friday someone told the story about how s/he came to live in Las Vegas and ultimately adjusted to living in this very unique community. Back in the spring I had written the story about how I had made Nevada home. It was an upbeat tale about my wonderful experiences working as a college instructor in Las Vegas. When I had returned from Europe in late July, I had dusted off the story and sent it in to KNPR. It was accepted, and they invited me to come to the studio to tape it.

On Friday, August 13, all those who tuned in heard me telling my tale. I explained how thrilled I had been to get offered a job at CCSN a year earlier. I spoke about my bringing in guest speakers and organizing internships. I told how I had spent a week in Washington with Shelley Berkley, and how Harry Reid had helped me to organize a trip for CCSN students to visit European political institutions. I told a story that was positive and inspiring, and I steered clear of the controversy that had cost me my job. I closed the segment with the following statement: "These activities are certainly glamorous. But the most rewarding aspect of my job is closer to home. It is when, after class, I step outside to find that my students are still discussing in the hall the political issues we'd examined in class. To know that I've had an impact on people's lives outside of the classroom — that's what really has made Nevada home for me."

Mike Green called to let me know that he'd heard me on the radio. "You did a great job," he said.

"Thanks," I replied. "I tried to keep it upbeat. It wasn't easy."

"You succeeded brilliantly. Listen, Lee, I thought that you should know something about your hiring. Remember last summer how Silverman was dragging his feet on offering you the job, despite the search committee's recommendation that he hire you?"

"Of course. Harry Reid and Kathy Von Tobel had to call before Silverman finally quit stalling."

"Did you ever wonder what had caused the delay?"

"Do *you* know?" I asked, my interest piqued.

"Yes, I do. The administration had gotten it into their heads that spring to hire a Hispanic for the political science position. Why exactly they thought they had to hire a second Hispanic political science instructor, I'm not sure. There were only four full-timers: two Caucasians (Larry and Al), one African American (Earnest), one Hispanic (Billy). If they really were interested in diversity, they should have hired a woman. But that's beside the point, of course. The fact is, they got it into their heads to hire a Hispanic, but no Hispanic who was good enough to make the cut applied for the job. At that point, they had two options, (1) to hire you, a white male with great credentials and a strong endorsement from a search committee — and both Earnest and Billy served on that committee — or (2) to cancel the search and start all over again. Silverman was seriously considering the latter option, when the senator's call tipped the balance in your favor."

"That's incredible!"

"That's not all. As soon as Silverman got rid of you, he told Charles that he'd better replace you with a woman."

So, apparently I was the victim of some sort of affirmative action gone haywire. That was pretty ironic, considering that I'd always been a strong supporter of recruiting a diverse faculty. It did not bother me so much that the administration might consider hiring a qualified minority instead of me. What irked me was that, apparently, it was preferable to hire no one at all, rather than hire a highly qualified white male. How bizarre.

A few days later I got a call from Tick. "Moore got your letter. Armstrong called and asked me, 'what do we have to give him so that he'll go away?'"

"What's that supposed to mean?" I asked.

"Armstrong didn't explain. Probably they want to offer you a lump sum to resign."

I scratched my head. "Does that mean they might be willing to give me more than one year's salary?

"It's possible, if you agreed to forego a lawsuit. But, actually, I doubt they'd agree to more than one year."

"Do I have a case, if I want to sue?"

"You can't sue for illegal firing. Nevada's an 'at-will employment' state. They don't need a reason to fire you. You *could* try to sue them for violating your First Amendment rights. But that would be a stretch."

"Not very promising, huh?"

"No."

I sighed. "Okay, Tick, do you think you could find out from Armstrong whether, if I agree not to sue, they might consider settling for more than the year's salary that I'm already entitled to?"

"Sure."

Tick got back to me a week later, on August 21. "I discussed the possibility of settlement with Armstrong. No way they'll settle for more than the year's salary you've already got. They want to give you less, in a lump sum, in exchange for a letter of recommendation from Moore."

I laughed. "Are they crazy? Why would I accept *less*?"

"These aren't Boy Scouts you're dealing with. When you go looking for another job, someone's going to call up your former employer. It's illegal for CCSN to divulge the details of why you left. But your potential employer might ask something like, 'Would you hire him again?' What do you think Silverman or Moore is going to answer?"

"Great!" I muttered despondently. "So, what do you advise?"

"More money is better than less. But it all depends on how much of a risk you're willing to take. It's your career."

"I wouldn't trust these guys, even if they gave me a letter of recommendation," I said. "For all I know, a letter from Moore would only make a potential employer even *more* likely to call him to check my references. Then what's to stop Moore from badmouthing me, despite his letter? No, I'll take my chances. No settlement."

"You're the boss."

Soon thereafter I received a letter from Dr. Silverman. He was apparently writing in response to my letter of July 27 to Richard Moore, in which I had requested an explanation of my firing and had told Moore that I wanted to receive my summer and overload pay.

Dear Mr. Miller:

Please be advised that all compensation due from the Community College of Southern Nevada has been paid to you. "Overload" teaching assignments are at the discretion of the administration of the Community College; therefore, there will be no money paid to you in regards to this issue.

Also, your appeal to President Moore regarding your request to rescind the "Notice of Non-Reappointment" has been denied. The reason for this denial has been previously communicated to you pursuant to the UCCSN Code.

Sincerely,

Robert M. Silverman, Ph.D.
Senior Vice President

"So," I thought, "I'm just going to have to be satisfied with no explanation other than a vague reference to 'unprofessional behavior.'" I noticed that Silverman had addressed the letter to "*Mr.* Miller," despite the fact that he had always called me *Dr.* Miller in the past. I could not help but think that he had done this as an intentional slight. I shrugged it off. He could take away my job, perhaps, by not my Ph.D.

On September 2, Fox-5 TV news interviewed me, along with several of the participants on the European trip. The story presented the trip in a very positive light. I made sure not to mention the controversy surrounding the travel stipends or my dismissal. On September 8, a story in a similar vein appeared in the *Las Vegas Sun*, the local evening newspaper.

On the evening of September 2, Billy Monkman gave me a call.

"Thanks a lot for standing up for me in the faculty meeting last month," I said. "Mike told me about it."

"I wish I could have done more."

I sighed. "Yeah, me too. But I really appreciate you trying."

"Al shot it down. He goes around telling people you're devious and manipulative."

"What's with him?"

"I don't know. He won't talk to me about you."

"Mike and Candace told me the same thing. But he shouldn't go around badmouthing me. I haven't done anything manipulative or devious — to Al or to anyone else."

After deliberating for a day, I decided to confront Al Balboni on this issue. I sent him the following e-mail.

Dear Alan,

As per your request in late May, I have not telephoned you. I must admit that I am totally mystified by your request. I had considered you to be a friend and a mentor. I have respected your wishes thus far, and I have asked for no explanation.

However, I have become increasingly disturbed as one colleague after another has told me that you have publicly called me "devious" and "manipulative" and other derogatory things. I believe that I deserve an explanation for this. I have always treated you and all other colleagues with the utmost respect. To my knowledge, I have done nothing to warrant such DEFAMATION OF CHARACTER.

I certainly hope that we can sort out, as gentlemen, whatever issue has irritated you.

Please call me.

Sincerely,

Lee Miller

On the same day, Al sent me the following reply: "That's the way it is." I had no idea what that was supposed to mean, but I did not bother to write back and ask him. Apparently, though, Al himself came to the conclusion that a further explanation was in order. Two

172

days later, on September 5, Al sent me another message. This time he made sure to cc Charles, Candace, and Silverman:

> Do not abuse the UCCSN e-mail system to communicate your malicious rantings. I have never defamed your name; indeed at a summer PRS Dept. meeting, I explicitly stated that i [sic] would not speak ill of you even though I applaude [sic] the decision to terminate you at CCSN. Indeed, the record shows further that I wished you well in subsequent professional endeavors.
>
> Shame on you for casting aspirtions [sic] on the small handful of PRS faculty who, in spite of any misgivings they might have about your boorish behavior, questioned the severity of the punishment.
>
> Do not contact me again.
>
> AB

I was depressed. I had put my heart and soul into my job at CCSN. I had worked sixty hours per week, when I could have gotten away with twenty. I had created all sorts of innovative programs, and had received a couple of grants in recognition of my work. In the end, Silverman apparently had fired me *because* of all this. Just like the Japanese proverb, the nail that sticks up ultimately gets hammered down.

My job prospects seemed grim. I had applied for hundreds of full-time jobs over the course of two years, and the job at CCSN was the only one that I had been offered. Now, I faced the prospect of starting the process all over, only this time I was handicapped by the fact that a former employer was likely to speak badly of my job performance.

I went to Spiritual Endeavors for the first time in many months. During the previous two semesters, my classes had conflicted with the time of the meetings. After the semester had ended, I had been too busy to go. Now that the European trip was past, and my contract with CCSN more or less settled, I was ready to return to Spiritual Endeavors.

Simon greeted me with a big bear hug. "How are you, Lee?" he asked.

"Terrible," I moaned. "This year, I've been working my ass off at CCSN. I brought in prominent politicians as guest speakers, I set up an internship program, I got a grant to spend a week in Congress, I led a trip to Europe where students met with European officials. I did a great job, and my students loved me. But the VP at the College fired me, and he won't even tell me why. I won't be able to teach next year, although because of my contract, they're still going to have to pay my salary."

Simon smiled. "Lee, that's wonderful!" he cried.

I looked at him as if he was crazy. "What are you talking about?"

"It's right before your eyes," he whispered gently, "if you'd only open them and look at it."

"What do you mean?" I snapped, stung by his lack of sympathy.

"Lee," he replied, taking no offense at my harsh tone of voice, "months ago you told me that you wished you had more time for writing. Now, look what you've created for yourself. A year in which you don't have to work, and can spend all your time writing. This is truly wonderful!"

I shook my head, bewildered.

"Think about it. Let's say you never lost your job. Did you have any time for writing up till this point?"

"No. I was too busy with all sorts of projects, like organizing the European trip, and —"

"Of course you were busy. You put everything you had into that job, didn't you?"

"And they fired me anyway!"

Simon held up his hand. "Imagine for a second that you still work at CCSN," he said. "You've finished all your projects this year. Now, ask yourself: are you going to have more free time next year? Or will you find some new projects to eat up all your time?"

I opened my mouth to argue the point, but I knew that he was right. I hated to admit it to myself, but I'd been working sixty hours per week *by choice*. I'd put my heart and soul into my job, always doing more than was expected. I always would have sought out some new challenge, once I had achieved the previous goal. That was my nature — or at least, that was the way I'd unconsciously run my life up till that point.

"Okay," I said at last. "I guess you're right. I've been a bit of a workaholic. But, Simon, I lost my job!"

"Lee, you didn't lose your job!" Simon cried, laughing. "You got a year's paid vacation!" He laid his hand on my shoulder. "Think about it. Say they just fired you, and gave you nothing. What would you do then?"

"I'd get another job. But —"

"Exactly. You'd get another job. Right away, I bet. And as a professor somewhere else —"

I shook my head. "No, I wouldn't get another job as a professor somewhere else. It's summertime. They hire college professors in the winter and spring for the following fall. No chance I'd get a job as a professor for this fall. It's too late." I clenched my right fist and slapped it angrily in the palm of my left hand. "I'd have to take a job doing something else. I'd wait tables or valet cars or God knows what else, just so that I could pay the rent!"

Simon remained unperturbed. "I guess you'd have to wait a lot of tables to make ends meet. Probably wouldn't have much time for writing."

I ground my teeth, and shook my head.

"And suppose you got a job with more responsibility. Say someone recognized your creativity and intelligence and offered you a great job doing something where you could make use of them. Say they hired you to head up some big project or something. You'd just slack off and take it easy, right?"

"Of course not! I'd give it 110%, like always. What's your point?"

"That *is* my point. If they hadn't fired you, you never would have found the time for your writing. If they had fired you without any severance pay, you would have found another job, and never would have found the time for writing. But they didn't do either of those things. In fact, they didn't really fire you at all. They gave you a year's paid vacation. What are you going to do with your time off? Take a trip around the world?"

I imagined myself traveling to Europe and Africa and Australia, all with Bob Silverman picking up the tab. "Tempting," I said, grinning. "But maybe I should get a job, and collect two salaries, so that I can pay off my student loans over the next year."

Simon shook his head. For the first time in our conversation, a hint of frustration entered his voice. "Lee, do you remember where this conversation began?"

I thought back. "I told you that I'd gotten fired."

"And I congratulated you on creating a situation where you'll have the time and the money to finish that book of yours."

"You're blaming *me* for getting fired?"

"No. I'm not blaming anyone. But you create your own reality. In your old reality — working at CCSN — you never had time for writing…."

My eyes opened wide. "And I never would have, if they hadn't fired me!" I gasped. I finally began to understand what Simon was talking about. "And if they had fired me without pay, I would have gotten a new job, and continued being a workaholic, and never would have found the time to write."

Simon nodded, grinning. "Instead, they gave you a year off with pay. What are you going to do with it?"

"Finish my book!" I hugged the big bear of a man. "Simon, you're amazing!" I cried. "Things have worked out perfectly, and I didn't even realize it! I have a year to work on my book, and they're going to pay me for it!"

Simon smiled. "I'm so proud of you, Lee," he said, giving me another hug. "You've come a long way."

I called Beth right away and let her know that I'd decided to join her in Los Angeles. She was thrilled. We found a beautiful apartment in Redondo Beach, a suburb of L.A. Every day I sat at my computer, gazing at the blue Pacific Ocean, working on my novel. I felt like I was the luckiest man in the world.

When I finished *Retsamdros*, I dedicated it to Bob Silverman, for giving me the time and resources to complete it, and to Simon, for helping me to see how truly blessed I was.

Epilogue

A lot has happened since I left Las Vegas. The newspapers have been bulging with stories about the principal characters in my tale. Here is a summary of what has happened to some of them, as of December 5, 2002:

My colleagues in the Department of Philosophical and Regional Studies
Soon after my departure from CCSN, Gary Elliott died of a heart attack. A scholarship was endowed in his honor.

Jim Fuller left CCSN for a job at a college in Indiana. The rest of my former colleagues remain at CCSN. Charles Okeke has been named interim dean of the Social Science Division. Fran Campbell was elected interim department chair. Al Balboni, Royse Smith, Candace Kant, Mark Rauls, Billy Monkman, and Mike Green all still teach at CCSN. Mike Green now also is a columnist for the *Las Vegas Mercury*.

Gertrude
Gertrude's fight with Silverman, apparently, had no serious repercussions in the long run. After graduation, Gertrude returned to CCSN to take some more classes, and she found another campus job. She went on to complete an additional degree.

Bill Cassell

Bill Cassell served a couple more years as associate vice president for international student programs at CCSN. He managed to stay out of the newspapers during that time. His budget for international student recruitment for the 1999–2000 academic year totaled $270,000.[1] He retired at the end of that academic year and returned to California.

Larry Braxton, Dave Abramson, Maurice Norrise, and the CCSN Student Government

In December 1999, security officers escorted Student Government advisor Larry Braxton off of campus. Braxton was asked to resign his post at CCSN after pleading guilty to fraud charges related to his previous position at a college in California. A March 2000 story in the *Coyote Press*,[2] the CCSN student newspaper, states that Braxton, who advised the Student Government on how to spend its annual budget of more than half a million dollars, was being investigated for possible wrongdoing at CCSN. Braxton, apparently, had been extremely liberal in giving out thousands of dollars worth of "vouchers" — paid for with Student Government funds — for dinners at restaurants, movie tickets, and entrance to amusement parks. No records were kept regarding whom the vouchers were given to.

On May 11, 2001, the *Coyote Press* reported that Braxton was still on the CCSN payroll, working as coordinator of the Retention and Persistence Program.[3] The story suggested that Braxton was able to retain his job due to "the support of one outspoken regent, and a top administrator at Cheyenne campus."

Braxton finally left CCSN for good at the end of his 2000–2001 contract, on June 30, 2001.

In July 2001, the *Las Vegas Sun* reported that a February 2000 audit of the CCSN Student Government found very sloppy record-keeping, in which some $185,000 was unaccounted for.[4] Students at CCSN had been paying a mandatory $2 fee to the Student Government for every credit hour they took at CCSN. This added up to a lot of money. The annual budget of the CCSN Student Government totaled approximately $580,000 for the 2001–2002 fiscal year. Around one-fourth of that amount was spent on parties, some costing as much as $25,000, most of which were not well attended.

Another $20,000 was spent on out of state trips for members of the Student Government, including one to Santa Barbara to see the musical "Showboat." Lunch bills exceeding $100 were quite common and tens of thousands of dollars of newly purchased office equipment could not be accounted for.

Despite this stinging report, and subsequent reforms in the advising structure for the Student Government, the abuses continued. The last straw, apparently, was reached in November 2001, when the Student Government spent $10,000 to go on a retreat in Primm, a resort town near the state line with California, rather than holding the retreat for free on campus.[5] On December 7, 2001, the Board of Regents voted to reduce CCSN Student Government funding to $0.50 per credit hour, the rate at all other community colleges in Nevada. The change was set to take effect at the beginning of the new fiscal year, in July 2002. Student fees were not scheduled to be reduced, however; the money taken from the Student Government was to be funneled instead into an account under the direct control of the college president.[6]

A March 2000 *Coyote Press* story indicates that in October 1999, Dave Abramson was forced to resign the presidency of the CCSN Student Government after being caught using Student Government money to buy clothing for himself. He was also accused of selling vouchers of the same sort that Braxton allegedly had been abusing.[7]

The *Coyote Press* reported on November 10, 2000, that on November 3, Shannon Schilling, the Student Government president, expelled Treasurer Maurice Norrise and two senators from the Student Government. Norrise, you may recall, was the student senator whom Braxton had denounced for supporting the proposal to provide scholarships for the European trip. Schilling took this action claiming that the members in question had not fulfilled the requirement to spend at least five hours per week in their posts. Emotions flared in response; one member of the Student Government walked out of the meeting, while the president ordered another removed from the room. A motion to reinstate Norrise failed.[8] An editorial in the same issue of the *Coyote Press* alleged that Schilling was behaving like a "dictator," and that the meeting had violated the Nevada Open Meetings Law. The editorial also scolded Schilling for giving himself and his vice president a 50% pay increase.[9] Some things never change, I suppose.

Richard Moore, Orlando Sandoval, and the Nevada State College at Henderson

Despite the misgivings of Regent Steve Sisolak, among others, the state of Nevada decided to take the first steps toward creating a new state college in Henderson, a southern suburb of Las Vegas. They budgeted more than half a million dollars to hire a founding president and for expenses related to planning the new institution. In a meeting behind closed doors in December 1999, the University and Community College System of Nevada (UCCSN) Board of Regents decided not to conduct a formal search and to offer the post of founding president to Richard Moore. According to newspaper reports, Regents Chair Jill Derby had changed the meeting time so that Regents Steve Sisolak and David Phillips — two Moore critics — would not be able to attend. The office of the state attorney general reprimanded the Regents for violating the state Open Meetings Law.[10]

Moore accepted the job. It included a big pay increase, bringing his annual salary to $175,000.

A short time after he was appointed, Moore hired Orlando Sandoval, CCSN vice president for planning and campus sites, for an equivalent position at Nevada State College. You may recall him as the "Orlando" who was chasing after Moore during my first meeting with the college president in 1997. Sandoval, who'd had no high school diploma until completing his GED just a short time earlier, saw his salary increased to $125,000 per year.[11] Needless to say, this hire put Moore over budget, as so often had been the case during his tenure at CCSN. The attorney general opened an investigation into Sandoval's appointment as well.

Next the press learned of a secret deal between Moore and former U.S. Senator Paul Laxalt.[12] A month before he was appointed president of the new college, Moore hired Laxalt for $10,000 per month to lobby Congress to provide funding for projects at CCSN. Not only was Moore criticized for extravagant spending in a time of tight budgets, but he also was slammed for keeping the deal secret. Moore had been courting the former senator for quite some time. A couple of years earlier, Moore had named the teacher education center at CCSN after Laxalt, and had hired Laxalt's daughter to serve as its director.

In April, the story broke that a year earlier Moore had hired a former Henderson city manager for $5,000 per month to lobby the state government. The *Las Vegas Review-Journal* also revealed that CCSN had donated $100,000 to the Henderson Chamber of Commerce for the creation of a small business support center.[13] Moore's critics claimed that he had been spending scarce CCSN resources in an effort to convince the state government to found a new college in Henderson — the college that he ultimately was appointed to head. Moore's spending had contributed to the fact that CCSN was over budget by some $774,000, three months before the end of the fiscal year. The college was forced to dip into reserves.

Later that month, a former CCSN employee filed a complaint with the state personnel department that he had been fired the previous November for questioning the legality and ethics of spending over $100,000 to purchase equipment to produce bronze busts of prominent politicians and college donors. The equipment had been used to produce busts of television executive Jim Rogers, Governor Kenny Guinn, and state Senate Majority Leader Bill Raggio. The fired employee later ended up suing the college.[14]

In June, a state audit found evidence of financial mismanagement during Moore's presidency at CCSN. The auditors found that more than half of the expenditures from the "host" account under Moore's control had no documentation, leaving them unable to determine whether the expenditures had been proper. Furthermore, the auditors found that, during the last few months of Moore's leadership, CCSN had exceeded its budget by $2.2 million, and had violated various state policies. The Department of Planning and Administrative Services, which Sandoval had headed until his plum appointment at Nevada State College, was so badly mismanaged that the department was abolished in response to the revelations.[15]

The next month, the press reported that Moore had donated tens of thousands of dollars of non-surplus college furniture and office equipment to various organizations. The equipment had included nine computers and three laser printers given to private organizations, several headed by Moore supporters. For more than a year, CCSN also had been paying the monthly bills for the phone lines providing Internet access for these computers.[16] The recipients of the computers included the local chapter of the American Association of Retired

Persons (headed by the wife of Regent David Phillips), the Latin Chamber of Commerce (headed by Orlando Sandoval), and the National Association for the Advancement of Colored People (NAACP). Both the Latin Chamber of Commerce and NAACP had lobbied the Regents to appoint Moore president of the new Nevada State College at Henderson. Regent Phillips, on the other hand, did not have a reputation as a Moore-booster, and some people speculated that the donation had represented an effort to curry favor.[17]

The donation of college computers was particularly ironic, given that the CCSN Student Government had been compelled to spend $140,000 its own money to provide computers for the libraries and student computer labs. Such expenditures should normally be the responsibility of the college administration. Both the UCCSN Chancellor's office and the state attorney general opened investigations into financial practices at CCSN under Moore and Silverman.

In September 2000, several new scandals came to light. CCSN faculty were outraged to learn that Moore had given tens of thousands of dollars in bonuses to four administrators during the previous two years, despite the fact that faculty had been denied a cost of living increase, ostensibly due to budgetary limitations. Furthermore, it was revealed that, over a five-year period, Moore had bypassed standard competitive search procedures and promoted selected administrators, giving them pay increases ranging from 39% to 152%. Over the same period average annual faculty pay increased by a meager 2.5%. Even more troubling, over the preceding year, 89% of administrative and faculty hires had been "emergency hires," leaving the administration open to charges of cronyism and nepotism, as family, friends, and politicians were hired without engaging in a competitive search process.[18]

In September 2000, newspapers reported that CCSN had overstated its enrollment figures by nearly 10%.[19] The more students enrolled at the college, the more state funding it was entitled to receive. It turned out that enrollment at CCSN had actually fallen by 5.4% in fall 2000, compared to a year earlier. CCSN was the only college in the state of Nevada to experience a significant fall in enrollment that semester. By February 2001, CCSN announced a hiring freeze in anticipation of a $16 million dollar budget cut, due to the drop in enrollment.

On October 20, 2000, UCCSN Chancellor Jane Nichols issued a report outlining the various abuses at CCSN under the administration of Moore and Silverman.[20] Nichols criticized practices at CCSN, and proposed new policies and safeguards to reduce the likelihood of such problems in the future. Steve Sisolak and another regent criticized the report, arguing that CCSN administrators should be held directly accountable for their actions. The *Las Vegas Review-Journal* blasted Nichols' mild response, calling the college system "Nevada's Tammany Hall."[21]

The same day, the Regents approved a budget of $549,512 for the yet-to-be-built Nevada State College at Henderson. This was a substantial increase over the previous year's budget. The majority of the money was earmarked for Moore's $175,000 salary and Sandoval's $125,000 salary. Moore was also slated to receive a $12,000 housing allowance, a $6,000 car allowance, and a $5,000 "host" fund. The state attorney general continued to investigate charges of wrongdoing by Moore, Sandoval, and the CCSN administration.

In March 2001, the state attorney general's office released a report of misdeeds under Moore's tenure at CCSN.[22] Charges included enrollment padding, inflated prices paid to contractors (contracts were not sent out for open bidding), lavish spending on office furniture by Moore (such as a $6,000 table and chairs with imported Italian fabric), and violations of the state anti-nepotism law by Orlando Sandoval.

Sandoval was alleged to have been "intimately involved" with the promotion and steady increase in salary of his own father-in-law. Sandoval's father-in-law had enjoyed a 43% salary increase over a four year period. New job titles were created on two occasions in order to facilitate the man's promotion. The salary increases exceeded college guidelines, requiring special permission from then-CCSN President Moore.

Sandoval was indicted by a state grand jury on June 28, 2001, and faced up to a year in prison.[23] The charges were later dismissed on a technicality, and the statute of limitations ran out before a second grand jury was able to convene.[24]

The attorney general reported that enrollment padding under Moore had included a scheme to rent union halls and hire union personnel to teach apprenticeship classes that union members needed to take, so that the union members could be counted toward college enrollment figures.[25]

The report also affirmed earlier allegations of bypassing normal search procedures for hiring of college personnel, as well as the payment of thousands of dollars in bonuses to college administrators. The bonuses were paid as rewards to administrators when the college exceeded enrollment growth targets. Federal law prohibits giving bonuses or other financial incentives for recruitment of students, and the U.S. Department of Education opened an investigation into the policy at CCSN. According to an article in the *Las Vegas Sun* dated April 12, 2001, if found in violation of this law, CCSN stands to lose federal funding equivalent to 5% of its annual budget.[26]

On April 30, 2001, Allen Ruter, CCSN vice president of finance and administration, died of a heart attack.

In June 2001, the Nevada state legislature voted to spend $13.4 million toward construction costs at the Nevada State College at Henderson, and $7 million in operating costs for the second year of operation. The legislature neglected to approve any money for the operation of the college during its first year, despite the fact that classes were scheduled to begin in fall 2002. This meant that there was no money in the budget to pay the salaries of Moore, Sandoval, and other administrators at the college. In Nevada, the state legislature meets for up to 120 days every other year, and was not scheduled to reconvene until 2003. In response to this problem, the Regents renewed Moore's contract for the next two years, but made his salary dependent on private sector donations to the planned college. The positions of Orlando Sandoval, as well as Joyce Tomlinson, Moore's secretary, remained unfunded, and both announced their retirement.[27]

Moore's salary was to be paid until the end of 2001 out of a donation from LandWell Corp. This company had previously offered to donate land for construction of the college in exchange for the annexation of a large tract of polluted land by the city of Henderson. City officials had rejected the offer, and instead agreed to sell a tract of city-owned land to the Regents for the construction of the college.

In August 2001, the Regents voted to ask the state legislature to lend them $700,000 from the state estate tax fund to pay the salaries of employees at the Nevada State College at Henderson. The legislature was not scheduled to reconvene again until 2003, and the Legislative Interim Finance Committee voted on September 25 to wait until November 2001 before considering the request. The members of the committee expressed concerns about the deterioration of the state's finances with the onset of recession, as well as the fact that donations to the new college had not met expectations.

On October 9, it was announced that several anonymous donors had given nearly half a million dollars to the college. The Regents withdrew their request for estate tax funds.

In February 2002, newspapers reported that Moore had been paying consultants $1,000 per day in salary, plus providing $500 per day expense accounts, for work related to setting up the new college. Regents Steve Sisolak and Tom Kirkpatrick criticized the fees as "exorbitant." They also criticized Moore for paying political consultant Kent Oram $8,570 per month to provide damage-control while the media reported on the many scandals with which Moore had been associated. UCCSN Chancellor Jane Nichols launched an investigation. The contracts had been executed without UCCSN oversight, and they were found to be very sloppy. For example, several contained inaccurate information, and the dates on several had been changed. Sisolak was quoted in the *Las Vegas Review-Journal* as saying, "The best case is that this is the same kind of mismanagement or ineptness we saw while Richard Moore was president of CCSN."[28]

On February 25, Moore resigned his $182,000 per year job as president of the yet-to-be-created Nevada State College. He requested a six-month leave of absence. The end of his leave of absence would coincide with the opening date of the new college, and Moore asked to be granted a position teaching business and economics at the institution.

The Regents unanimously voted to offer Moore a tenured faculty position. To start, they gave Moore a nine-month, $90,000 contract, set to begin on July 1, 2002. They also approved Moore's request for a six-month leave of absence, and decided to continue paying Moore's $182,000 annual salary until the start of his new contract.[29]

The Regents appointed Chris Chairsell, UCCSN associate vice chancellor for academic and student affairs, to replace Moore as interim president of Nevada State College. Unlike Moore, the bulk of

Chairsell's salary did not come from private donations. The taxpayers picked up most of the bill. Chairsell took a paid leave of absence from her job with the state college system, and continued to collect her $114,446 annual salary, according to newspaper reports.[30] On top of that, she received $17,167 from the pool of donor money that had funded Moore's salary.[31]

Chairsell had served in a number of administrative posts under Moore at CCSN, rising rapidly up the ranks, before assuming her post with the statewide college system. You may remember her as the provost who escorted Gertrude off campus when Gertrude had confronted Silverman over her firing.

The Regents conducted a search for a more permanent president of Nevada State College at Henderson. On August 15 they voted to hire Kerry Romesburg, president of Utah Valley State College. He assumed the new position one month later. The Regents voted to pay Romesburg a base salary of $195,000, plus an allowance of $28,000 for housing, car, and entertainment expenses.[32]

On Tuesday, September 3, classes finally began at the Nevada State College at Henderson. They were held in a former vitamin warehouse and at several high schools. Only 177 students enrolled, out of the 380 who were admitted. The college had aimed for an incoming class of 500 full-time students. The legislature had authorized a budget of $3.75 million.[33]

Bob Silverman and the search for a new president of CCSN

After Moore's departure from CCSN in January 2000, to the Nevada State College at Henderson, Bob Silverman was promoted to interim president of CCSN, a job with an annual salary of $140,000. The Regents opened a nationwide search for a permanent CCSN president, and Silverman applied for the job.

On August 6, 2000, they announced that Silverman was not among the finalists. On August 25, in response to pressure from CCSN faculty, the Regents decided to add Silverman to the list of finalists.

On September 28, 2000, Bob Silverman withdrew himself from consideration for the post, citing insufficient support on the Board of Regents for his candidacy.[34] Rumors spread by faculty members suggested that Moore, who had the support of a majority of regents, had pressured the Regents to abandon his former lieutenant. Regardless of whether or not this was true, Silverman began looking for another job.

On April 1, 2001, Silverman left CCSN to assume the presidency of Mt. Hood Community College in Oregon. CCSN Athletic Director Michael Meyer was appointed Silverman's successor as interim CCSN president.

On September 27, the day before Silverman removed his name from consideration, the *Las Vegas Review-Journal* filed suit to force the Regents to hold public interviews of the finalists, rather than closed-door interviews, as they had planned. Refusing to conduct open interviews, the Board of Regents chose to fight the lawsuit, and decided to put off the final selection of CCSN's new president until the lawsuit was settled. The Regents lost the suit, and appealed to the state Supreme Court. The high court overturned the lower court ruling, allowing the interviews to be conducted behind closed doors. But the Regents decided to start the search from scratch, and to hold public interviews after all.[35] The first person offered the job by the Regents, in May 2001, turned it down.[36] On June 8, the Regents voted to offer the job to Ron Remington, president of Great Basin College in northern Nevada. Remington accepted, and assumed the presidency of CCSN in August 2001. Meyer resumed his post as CCSN Athletics Director.

Just three weeks later, on August 30, Meyer was forced to resign. He quit after making a racial slur within earshot of the wife of Wendell Williams, the chair of the State Assembly Education Committee. According to newspaper reports, when a colleague told Meyer in the hallway that he could not talk because he had an appointment with Mrs. Williams, Meyer replied, "Don't worry, niggers are always late." Mrs. Williams was on time, in fact sitting in the next room. Both Assemblyman Williams and his wife are African Americans.[37]

The author

During my year off with pay, I applied for political science instructor positions at various colleges. Apparently, my many accomplishments at CCSN made me a very appealing candidate. I was deluged with requests for job interviews from around the country. Eventually, I accepted a position at Cypress College in southern California. The job included a 42% salary increase over what I had been earning at CCSN.

Happy endings, of course, occur only in fairy tales. Cypress, I found, was not entirely free of tyrannical administrators or back-stabbing colleagues. But that is a story for another book.

Cast of Characters

Abramson, Dave: CCSN Student Government treasurer. Later elected to succeed Niecey Ransey as president.

Agnello, Todd: Miller's student. Worked as a Ferengi at the Star Trek Experience.

Ai Vi: Pseudonym for a CCSN student who worked as an exotic dancer.

Armstrong, Karl: Assistant general counsel, University and Community College System of Nevada.

Balboni, Alan "Al": CCSN political science professor. Chair of the Faculty Senate.

Berkley, Shelley: Regent, University and Community College System of Nevada. Later elected U.S. congresswoman. Miller received a grant to spend a week "shadowing" her as she performed her duties in Washington, DC.

Braxton, Larry: CCSN Student Government advisor.

Campbell, Fran: CCSN history instructor.

Cassell, William "Bill": CCSN associate vice president for international student programs. Gertrude's boss.

Chadwick, Calvin "Cal": Miller's student. Spearheaded lobbying of CCSN Student Government in favor of travel stipends for students participating in the European trip.

Chairsell, Chris: Provost of the West Charleston campus of CCSN.

Derby, Jill: Chair of Board of Regents, University and Community College System of Nevada.

Elliott, Gary: CCSN history professor.

Elez, Razije: Miller's student. Ethnic Albanian woman from Yugoslavia who applied for a travel stipend to go on the European trip.

Foreman, Linda: CCSN sociology professor. President of the Nevada Faculty Alliance, the professional association representing the interests of faculty with the CCSN administration and with government officials. Miller was a member of NFA.

Fuller, James: CCSN history instructor. Niecey Ransey's instructor.

Gatbonton, Dennis: Miller's student. One of three students who produced a video on homelessness in Las Vegas.

Gertrude: Pseudonym for an elderly woman who was a CCSN student. Eager promoter of the European trip.

Green, Michael "Mike": CCSN history professor. Contributor to *Las Vegas City Life*.

Guinn, Kenny: Governor of Nevada.

Gunther, Kurt: Miller's student. One of three students who produced a video on homelessness in Las Vegas.

Jacks, Joel: Miller's student. One of three students who produced a video on homelessness in Las Vegas.

James, Mark: Nevada state senator. Wrote a letter to the CCSN Student Government in support of the travel stipend proposal.

John: Pseudonym for a CCSN adjunct political science instructor.

Kant, Candace: CCSN history professor. Succeeded Al Balboni as chair of the Faculty Senate.

Laxalt, Paul: Former U.S. senator. Hired by Moore as a lobbyist.

Leichty, Mark: Miller's student. Ran for president of CCSN Student Government. Was defeated by Dave Abramson.

Littlepage, Marion "Page": CCSN dean of curriculum and scheduling.

Monkman, Guillermo "Billy": CCSN political science professor. Served on selection committee for travel stipends.

Moore, Richard: President of CCSN. Later appointed founding president of Nevada State College at Henderson.

Norrise, Maurice: CCSN Student Government senator. Later elected treasurer.

Nyamekye, Kwasi: Assistant general counsel, University and Community College System of Nevada.

Okeke, Charles: CCSN economics professor. Chair of Department of Philosophical and Regional Studies.

Patton, Natalie: *Las Vegas Review-Journal* reporter who authored a series of articles about scandals at CCSN.

Phillips, David: Regent, University and Community College System of Nevada.

Ransey, Sandra "Niecey": CCSN Student Government president.

Rauls, Mark: CCSN philosophy instructor. Served on selection committee for travel stipends.

Ray, Tom: General counsel, University and Community College System of Nevada.

Reid, Harry: U.S. senator. Miller's girlfriend worked as his aide.

Ruter, Alan: CCSN vice president for finance and administration.

Sally: Pseudonym for a CCSN student who went on the European trip.

Sandoval, Orlando: CCSN vice president for planning and campus sites. Hired by Moore for an equivalent position at Nevada State College at Henderson.

Schilling, Norman "Norm": Miller's student. Lead groundskeeper, Desert Demonstration Gardens, Las Vegas Metropolitan Water District.

Segerblom, Gene: Nevada state assemblywoman. Mother of Tick Segerblom.

Segerblom, Richard "Tick": Well-known labor lawyer. Miller's attorney. Son of Gene Segerblom.

Shaffer, Raymond: Nevada state senator. Participant on the European trip.

Silverman, Robert "Bob": CCSN senior vice president.

Sisolak, Steve: Regent, University and Community College System of Nevada.

Smith, Royse: CCSN political science professor. Preceded Al Balboni as chair of the Faculty Senate.

Stops, Arlie: CCSN assistant vice president for admissions and records. Mentor to Gertrude.

Story, Tod: Congresswoman Berkley's local office manager.

Taylor, Nathan: CCSN student. State Senator Mark James' local office manager. Vocal supporter of travel stipend proposal.

Turner, George: Miller's student. Retired Air Force non-commissioned officer.

Vandever, Judy: Clark County Recorder.

Von Tobel, Kathy: Miller's former student. Nevada state assemblywoman. Recommended Miller for full-time job at CCSN.

Washington, Tanya: Miller's student. Worked as an intern for Senator Reid. Ran unsuccessfully for CCSN Student Government.

White, David: CCSN student. Participant on the European trip. Former Americorps volunteer.

Index

Notes

Chapter 4

[1] See the following articles from the *Las Vegas Review-Journal:* Mike Zapler, "Officials examine waste company," January 18, 1999; Keith Rogers, "Panel uphold violation against Western Elite for illegal dump," May 3, 1999; Mike Zapler, "City Council postpones OK of sludge pact," November 4, 1999; Mike Zapler, "Sludge law seen outdated," November 16, 1999; Mike Zapler, "City Council delays sludge pact vote," February 17, 2000; Mike Zapler, "Council takes flak for Silver State sludge deal," March 2, 2000.

Chapter 6

[1] Natalie Patton, "CCSN's foreign student program raises questions," *Las Vegas Review-Journal*, August 1, 1997.

[2] See the following *Las Vegas Review-Journal* articles by Natalie Patton: "CCSN's foreign student program raises questions" (August 1, 1997); "College official navigates globe at public's expense" (August 6, 1997); "Foreign recruitment questioned" (August 8, 1997); "Community college assembles task force to explore recruiting" (August 9, 1997); "Foreign student program backed" (November 6, 1997); "Regents to review foreign program" (December 4, 1997); "Overseas recruiting by college criticized" (December 14, 1997); "Community college seeks foreign tuition exemption" (September 11, 1997); "Panel: Keep recruiters at home" (September 25, 1997). See also Sean Waley, "Foreign student program urged to resume," *Las Vegas Review-Journal*, December 5, 1997. Cassell wrote an op-ed piece in response to Patton's reporting: William K. Cassell, "Foreign recruitment an example of administrative vision," *Las Vegas Review-Journal*, August 13, 1997. The *Las Vegas Review-Journal*

also ran two editorials critical of Cassell's overseas recruitment efforts. See "On the road again" (August 5, 1997) and "Globe-trotting at CCSN" (August 8, 1997). CCSN political science professor Larry Tomlinson responded to these editorials: "Community college is more than a trade school," *Las Vegas Review-Journal*, August 29, 1997.

Chapter 8

[1] See the following articles by Natalie Patton in the *Las Vegas Review-Journal:* "Costly college busts missing" (April 21, 2000), and "Whistle-blower to forgo hearing" (August 12, 2000). See also Michael Green "No Moore," *Las Vegas City Life*, April 27, 2000.

[2] Geoff Schumacher, "College gets attention with billboard message," *Las Vegas City Life*, August 12, 1999.

Epilogue

[1] Natalie Patton, "Campus foreign program costly," *Las Vegas Review-Journal*, April 6, 2000. See also the April 9, 2000 editorial in the *Las Vegas Review-Journal*, "Foreign accounting at CCSN."

[2] Denise Jaramillo, "Student advisor fired after felony guilty plea in Calif.," *Coyote Press*, March 2000.

[3] Nick Lane, "Convicted felon Larry Braxton runs retention program at CCSN," *Coyote Press*, May 11, 2001.

[4] See the following articles by Jennifer Knight in the *Las Vegas Sun:* "Student fees going to parties: Audit slams expenses of CCSN student government leaders" (July 13, 2001) and "Regents weigh CCSN oversight" (July 30, 2001). See also the editorial in the *Las Vegas Sun* on July 13, 2001: "Government leaders abuse students' trust."

[5] Jennifer Knight, "CCSN student government funding still a concern," *Las Vegas Sun*, November 5, 2001.

[6] Jennifer Knight, "CCSN student body to receive less funding," *Las Vegas Sun*, December 10, 2001. See also the editorial in the *Las Vegas Sun* on December 11, 2001: "Spending that is out of control."

[7] Denise Jaramillo, "Student advisor fired after felony guilty plea in Calif.," *Coyote Press*, March 2000.

[8] Kathleen Mondino, "Student Government Turns into a Battle of Wills," *Coyote Press*, November 18, 2000.

[9] Babette May-Herrmann, "November 3, 2000 Student Government meeting: Chicanery at its height of absurdity," *Coyote Press*, November 18, 2000.

[10] Michael Green, "No Moore," *Las Vegas City Life*, April 27, 2000.

[11] Michael Green, "Moore of the same," *Las Vegas City Life*, March 30, 2000.

[12] Natalie Patton, "Lobbying firm drops college," *Las Vegas Review-Journal*, March 17, 2000. See also the March 19, 2000 editorial in the *Las Vegas Review-Journal*: "Expensive hired help."

[13] Natalie Patton, "Moore criticized for spending," *Las Vegas Review-Journal*, April 15, 2000.

[14] See the following articles by Natalie Patton in the *Las Vegas Review-Journal*: "Costly college busts missing" (April 21, 2000),

and "Whistle-blower to forgo hearing" (August 12, 2000). See also Michael Green, "No Moore," *Las Vegas City Life*, April 27, 2000.

[15] Sean Whaley, "College responds to audit," *Las Vegas Review-Journal*, June 21, 2000; Ed Vogel, "Regent demands more accountability," *Las Vegas Review-Journal*, June 24, 2000. In addition, see the June 23, 2000 editorial in the *Las Vegas Review-Journal*, "Technical in nature."

[16] See the following articles by Natalie Patton in the *Las Vegas Review-Journal:* "Regents critical of computer donations" (July 4, 2000), "Internal computer inquiry launched" (July 7, 2000), "AARP returns loaned PCs" (July 14, 2000), "Latin chamber returning computers to CCSN" (July 22, 2000), "NAACP to return college's computers" (July 27, 2000), and "More CCSN freebies revealed" (September 2, 2000). See also two editorials in the *Las Vegas Review-Journal:* "PCs for the people?" (July 7, 2000) and "College computer giveaway" (July 17, 2000). In addition, see Sean Whaley, "Computer loan causes outrage," *Las Vegas Review Journal*, August 12, 2000; and Lisa Kim Bach, "Property-lending practices remain on CCSN's agenda," *Las Vegas Review Journal*, September 9, 2000.

[17] See the July 17, 2000 editorial in the *Las Vegas Review-Journal:* "College computer giveaway."

[18] Michael Green, "Dim and Dimmer," *Las Vegas City Life*, July 6, 2000; Natalie Patton, "CCSN employee bonuses criticized," *Las Vegas Review-Journal*, September 24, 2000; Cy Ryan, "Regents want answers from CCSN leaders," *Las Vegas Sun,* October 23, 2000.

[19] Patton, Natalie. September 16, 2000. "CCSN Enrollment: Regents question counting practices." See also September 19,

2000 editorial in the *Las Vegas Review-Journal*, "And now... phantom students."

[20] Cy Ryan, "CCSN gets mixed reviews in report," *Las Vegas Sun*, October 20, 2000.

[21] "Nevada's Tammany Hall," editorial in *Las Vegas Review-Journal*, October 20, 2000. This is an allusion to the notoriously corrupt political machine dominating the city of New York from the 1860s until the 1940s.

[22] See the following articles by Jennifer Knight in the *Las Vegas Sun*: "CCSN officials scrutinized" (March 23, 2001) and "Regents to question Moore in closed session" (April 13, 2001).

[23] See the following articles by Jennifer Knight in the *Las Vegas Sun*: "Former CCSN official faces charges" (June 29, 2001), "Sandoval arraignment set Aug. 2" (July 3, 2001), and "CCSN salary case unfolds" (July 25, 2001).

[24] Cy Ryan, "High court rules in favor of former CCSN administrator," *Las Vegas Sun*, January 18, 2002.

[25] Cy Ryan and Ed Koch, "University system grew too quickly, official says," *Las Vegas Sun*, March 20, 2001.

[26] Jennifer Knight, "Feds to investigate CCSN bonus program," *Las Vegas Sun*, April 12, 2001.

[27] See the following articles by Jennifer Knight in the *Las Vegas Sun*: "Moore, top aide, left without funding for pay" (June 12, 2001), and "State college official resigns" (June 28, 2001).

[28] Natalie Patton, "Nevada State College at Henderson: Chancellor's office to review contracts," *Las Vegas Review-*

Journal, February 16, 2002. See also the February 19, 2002 editorial in the *Las Vegas Review-Journal*, "Contract oversight."

[29] Associated Press, "Moore resigning as head of yet-to-open college in Henderson," *Las Vegas Sun*, February 26, 2002; Jennifer Knight, "College's future in doubt after president resigns," *Las Vegas Sun*, February 26, 2002; Natalie Patton, "Surprise resignation: College's president quits post," *Las Vegas Review-Journal*, February 26, 2002.

[30] Jennifer Knight, "Vice chancellor touted for interim college post," *Las Vegas Sun*, March 5, 2002.

[31] Jennifer Knight, "Interim president named for new college," *Las Vegas Sun*, March 8, 2002.

[32] Cy Ryan and Jennifer Knight, "President appointed for Henderson college," *Las Vegas Sun*, August 16, 2002. See also the August 18, 2002 column by Thomas Mitchell, editor of the *Las Vegas Review-Journal*, "Stand and deliver, knaves."

[33] Associated Press, "New Nevada college in Henderson begins classes," *Las Vegas Sun*, September 3, 2002. Jennifer Knight, "Nevada's first state college opens its doors," *Las Vegas Sun*, September 3, 2002.

[34] Natalie Patton, "Personnel search: Silverman won't seek CCSN post," *Las Vegas Review-Journal*, September 29, 2000.

[35] Jennifer Knight, "Search for CCSN chief starts over," *Las Vegas Sun*, March 12, 2001.

[36] Jennifer Knight, "CCSN chief runner-up expresses doubts," *Las Vegas Sun*, May 22, 2001.

[37] Steve Kanigher and Jeffrey Libby, "CCSN official quits over remark," *Las Vegas Sun*, August 31, 2001.

About the Author

LEE RYAN MILLER has taught political science and econimics for more than a decade at colleges and universities in the United States and Japan. He is the author of two political science books. He also has written two epic fantasy novels (as yet unpublished). He resides in Modesto, California. For more information, visit his website: www. LeeRyanMiller.com

Printed in the United States
28179LVS00002B/139-156